Athlone French Poets

JOSE-MARIA DE HEREDIA

Les Trophées

Athlone French Poets

General Editor EILEEN LE BRETON
Reader in French Language and Literature,
Bedford College, University of London

Monographs

GERARD DE NERVAL
THEOPHILE GAUTIER
HEREDIA
VERLAINE
RIMBAUD
JULES LAFORGUE
PAUL VALERY
GUILLAUME APOLLINAIRE
SAINT-JOHN PERSE
FRANCIS PONGE
HENRI MICHAUX

Critical Editions

VICTOR HUGO : CHATIMENTS
GERARD DE NERVAL : LES CHIMERES
ALFRED DE MUSSET : CONTES D'ESPAGNE ET D'ITALIE
THEOPHILE GAUTIER : POESIES
JOSE-MARIA DE HEREDIA : LES TROPHEES
PAUL VERLAINE : SAGESSE
PAUL VERLAINE : ROMANCES SANS PAROLES
ARTHUR RIMBAUD : LES ILLUMINATIONS
JULES LAFORGUE : LES COMPLAINTES
PAUL VALERY : CHARMES OU POEMES
GUILLAUME APOLLINAIRE : ALCOOLS
SAINT-JOHN PERSE: EXIL
PONGE: LE PARTI PRIS DES CHOSES
MICHAUX : AU PAYS DE LA MAGIE

JOSE-MARIA DE HEREDIA

Les Trophées

edited by

W. N. INCE

THE ATHLONE PRESS

1979

Published by
THE ATHLONE PRESS
at 4 Gower Street, London wc1

Distributed by
Tiptree Book Services Ltd
Tiptree, Essex

U.S.A. and Canada
Humanities Press Inc
New Jersey

© *W. N. Ince* 1979

British Library Cataloguing in Publication Data
Heredia, José-Maria de
Les trophées. – (Athlone French poets).
I. Title   II. Ince, Walter Newcombe
841′.8   PQ2275.H3T7
ISBN 0 485 14709 2 *cloth*
ISBN 0 485 12709 1 *paperback*

Printed in Great Britain by
Western Printing Services Limited
Bristol

Athlone French Poets

General Editor EILEEN LE BRETON

This series is designed to provide students and general readers both with Monographs on important nineteenth- and twentieth-century French poets and Critical Editions of one or more representative works by these poets.

The Monographs aim at presenting the essential biographical facts while placing the poet in his social and intellectual context. They contain a detailed analysis of his poetical works and, where appropriate, a brief account of his other writings. His literary reputation is examined and his contribution to the development of French poetry is assessed, as is also his impact on other literatures. A selection of critical views and a bibliography are appended.

The critical Editions contain a substantial introduction aimed at presenting each work against its historical background as well as studying its genre, structure, themes, style, etc. and highlighting its relevance for today. The text normally given is the complete text of the original edition. It is followed by full commentaries on the poems and annotation of the text, including variant readings when these are of real significance.

E. Le B.

CONTENTS

ROME ET LES BARBARES

Contents

LE MOYEN AGE ET LA RENAISSANCE

Contents

INTRODUCTION

A trophy is a memorial of victory, a captured standard, a monument or prize. So the title, *Les Trophées*, carries two implications: the poems are frequently concerned with impressive achievements or moments in history, and they also represent Heredia's own achievements, his linguistic capture of past events. To important, brilliant or picturesque times in the past he has set up monuments in words. His pleasure and justification when writing his poems were essentially aesthetic: for him and for us, with precision and suggestion, the past is evoked in fine language.

He seems to have formed the idea of a volume of poems as early as 1866 (Ibrovac, i, p. 302). It was to be called *Fleurs de feu*, after the title of one of his early sonnets. It is difficult to know for certain what he intended to include under that heading (perhaps influenced, but in name alone, by Baudelaire's *Fleurs du mal*). *Fleurs de feu* may have implied exotic and incandescent poems of exceptional intensity, located in hot climates and figuring only effulgent heroes, a much more restricted subject and treatment than the eventual volume was to offer. The title, *Les Trophées*, was probably suggested by Catulle Mendès (Ibrovac, i, p. 302). In a letter to Mallarmé on 11 April 1872, Heredia mentions this title for a volume of poems which he says he will perhaps publish some time in the next ten years.[1] He no doubt recalled the two old collections of sonnets *Les Trophées de la foi* (1591) by Du Bartas and *Les Trophées du roy* (1594) by Jean Godart. His own collection first appeared in 1893. It was immediately a great success, selling very quickly and in big numbers for that time. The reviews were completely favourable. But the poems had been composed over a period of thirty years; all but six of the sonnets had been published—often several times and slightly modified—in periodicals, reviews and collections. (Fifteen sonnets were not taken up in the first edition of *Les Trophées*. For details, see Ibrovac, i, p. 306, note 2.). In this way and through Heredia's enthusiastic recitations in society, many of his sonnets were known to a cultured public long before the appearance of *Les Trophées*. Gathering them into a book served several purposes. Most obviously, it satisfied an understandable desire to have his own volume that would set the seal on his distinctive contribution to French poetry. It pleased those friends and admirers who had long requested the opportunity to enjoy all his sonnets in a readily available form. Perhaps most importantly, as his preface reveals, his volume was a tribute to his friend and mentor, Leconte de Lisle:

> C'est pour vous complaire que je recueille mes vers épars. Vous m'avez assuré que ce livre, bien qu'en partie inachevé, garderait néanmoins aux yeux du lecteur indulgent quelque chose de la noble ordonnance que j'avais rêvée. Tel qu'il est, je vous l'offre, non sans regret de n'avoir pu mieux faire, mais avec la conscience d'avoir fait de mon mieux.

If one looks at *Les Trophées* as a collection, Heredia's modesty is understandable. Its structure was present in germ in the themes and order of the twenty-five sonnets published in the third *Parnasse contemporain* (1876), though the implicit sections had no headings. In 1893, Heredia is reasonably successful in his attempt to give his poems an appearance of system and unity by putting them under various headings: 'La Grèce et la Sicile', 'Rome et les Barbares', 'Le Moyen Age et la Renaissance', 'L'Orient et les tropiques', 'La Nature et le rêve', 'Romancero' and 'Les Conquérants de l'or'. The sonnets of a given section do mostly relate to its general theme. The risk of creating monotony by such a collection of poems in the same fixed form is partly averted by the very variety of the sections. And some variety amidst unity is obtained by Heredia's fondness for grouping his sonnets into diptychs and triptychs.[2] In his presentation Heredia was influenced by the preoccupations and artistic conventions of his time: the nineteenth century in France brought a remarkable flowering of historical studies and the historical vista in the form of an epic of humanity fascinated many nineteenth-century poets, most notably Hugo and Leconte de Lisle. Small wonder that François Coppée should describe *Les Trophées* as 'une sorte de *Légende des siècles* en sonnets'.[3] But only a little reflection is needed to realize what gaps there are in Hugo's *Légende des siècles*. And by comparison with Hugo and perhaps even more with Leconte de Lisle's *Poèmes antiques* (1852) and *Poèmes barbares* (1862), Heredia's collection is far from comprehensive. Thus there is little concerning the history of France, nothing on Scandinavia or Germany, nothing on India (possibly out of respect for Leconte de Lisle who devoted his attention so eruditely to Scandinavia and India). Heredia's classifications are far from being entirely satisfactory. The sections on Greece and Rome seem to have a chronological slant while 'L'Orient et les tropiques' is more a geographical division. 'La Nature et le rêve' is a curious mixture, following neither chronological nor geographical bent; into this part Heredia places anything remotely personal in inspiration or expression. If he must be defended against charges of so-called incompleteness, it need only be said that he was a poet, not a teacher: *Les Trophées* was neither intended to be nor is a history lesson. It might be thought that any intelligent and sensitive artist of French upbringing would necessarily desire a 'noble order' for his work. If Heredia did not quite achieve his dream, the loss is not really great. Despite the influences he underwent and the views others have taken of his collection, its title does not convey any explicitly or pretentiously epic implications; by its concrete plural, its emphasis is on the uniqueness of the separate trophies. If his book is to some extent, as he says, 'inachevé', along the lines suggested, it is supremely consummate at the level that matters, that of each sonnet. The individual sonnet was originally, in composition, and remains for us, the important unity: an integral vision or evocation.

Despite their universally favourable reception in 1893, *Les Trophées* could be regarded as being already in a sense out-of-date at that time. Verlaine, Mallarmé and Rimbaud, for instance, though not well known outside literary circles, had by then composed their best work. The Parnassian movement no longer held the centre of poets' attention. Symbolism had come and, to judge by the reactions of poets like Moréas, would soon be gone. Such considerations help us to recall how much *Les Trophées* are the splendid culmination of a line of poetic development which, if we set aside the importance to Heredia of poets like Ronsard and Chénier, begins with the first wave of Romantic poets at the beginning of the century and the Victor Hugo of *Les Orientales* (1829), passes through the art-for-art movement and poets like Gautier and Banville—who reacted against the first generation of Romantic poets—to reach its high point in *Le Parnasse* and Leconte de Lisle. *Les Trophées* are full of reminiscences of poetic predecessors, such as Banville.[4] Like many great poets of the past,

Heredia so admired such predecessors that he lovingly absorbed their work. He was happy to take them as his models, compete with them and, by his own efforts, often surpass them. He rarely failed to improve on the borrowings he made. Like the great Baudelaire, he habitually made something better and quite his own of such borrowings, or more accurately, such absorptions. His values as a poet have much in common with the ideas of the Parnassian movement and of poets like Gautier and Leconte de Lisle. Seen in negative terms, they are represented by the relative absence from *Les Trophées* of preoccupations with society, morality or contemporary issues, or even ideas as such. With rare exceptions, the poet's own personality, thoughts and emotions find no explicit mention. Effusiveness is entirely avoided. Though a 'philosophy' or attitude to life can be and has been deduced from *Les Trophées*, it is there only to the extent that any literary work must imply some view of life. If we consider Heredia's values in positive terms, *Les Trophées* can be seen as impersonal paintings of the past, a picturesque pageant, 'a series of historical cartoons'[5] where we are reminded of those watchwords of the art-for-art movement, *la beauté formelle, la beauté plastique*. He is usually less concerned to affect his readers' hearts, as many poets have done, by devoting himself directly and explicitly to certain 'big', 'human', themes—love, suffering, death—than to stir their imagination and sensitivity. One may have doubts concerning the facile opposition between moving 'hearts' and stirring 'senses'; the better viewpoint is perhaps that Heredia moves us *in his way* and in his chosen fields. But to criticize him, as some have done, for not 'moving the reader's heart' in the traditional manner seems pointless when it is appreciated that it was not his main aim to do so. Such restriction as his poetic genius reveals is both voluntary and superbly exploited. His impersonality and reserve are in accord with the very controlled composition of his poems.

Being financially independent, he was able to devote his life to his own interests: art and erudition. Poetry was his first and overriding passion but his early training at the *Ecole des Chartes* in Paris, though it led to no remunerated career in the traditional manner, set the stamp on a wide range of life-long pursuits: history and especially ancient history, archaeology, sculpture, numismatology, philology, painting, to mention the most important. His knowledge in these fields was that of the gifted and informed amateur, in the best sense of the term, knowledge comprehending technical details and skills. The evidence of these interests is present throughout *Les Trophées*, not just in the subjects treated but in the precision of detail often shown (e.g. the celebrated *mot juste*) and even more often implied. Beauty expressed in concrete form—a poem, a rare edition, a coin, a painting, a sculpture or a medieval sword—was his permanent preoccupation. Poets like Gautier are famous for their *transpositions d'art*, the expression of one art's aims or ideals in the medium of another. Heredia was the transposer *par excellence*: his sonnets are verbal depictions of the visual, palpable beauty he found and cherished in many fields of human endeavour.

It is therefore understandable that *Les Trophées* should present some difficulties to the modern reader. Few of us now have what used to be called a classical culture. Heredia read Greek and Latin fluently, he had an intimate and loving acquaintance with Greek and Latin literature. Few modern readers have acquired from early years that easy, detailed familiarity with mythological or historical heroes which was common among many of our forefathers and which so informs sections of *Les Trophées* like 'La Grèce et la Sicile' or 'Rome et les Barbares'. Some of Heredia's technical terms oblige a cultured Frenchman of today to reach for his dictionary, so the English reader will certainly expect to do no less. This edition does not seek to replace dictionaries but it will be my aim to explain those details, mythological, technical or aesthetic, which might stand in the way of the reader's understanding and so try to help him to lose any sense of alienation and savour the artistic achievement of *Les Trophées*. My later commentaries will be useful at the level of the individual sonnet. At this stage, my main concern is the general background to the various sections.

The first and last sonnets of *Les Trophées* provide an obvious frame for the whole collection. Both depict ruins, the first of some temple, the second of an ancient god. In both cases, though modern man is seen as indifferent to past civilizations, a poetic conceit makes nature kind to them, in 'L'Oubli' renewing the broken columns each spring with a fresh green, in 'Sur un marbre brisé' giving new life to the debris of the god's statue with leaves and light and shade. 'L'Oubli' develops a commonplace: the transitoriness of human achievements symbolized by the

statues of ancient gods and heroes lying in the grass amid the
ruins of the temple and against the background of unchanging
natural forces. Heredia discreetly laments the passing of past
beliefs and opens on a perspective which anticipates both the
subject and tone of the whole book. Like Leconte de Lisle, he is
to resurrect the past, but not to promulgate any deep philosophy
nor to arouse partisan feelings: 'L'Oubli' seems predomi-
nantly pictorial, but both its sound and tone as well as its subject
help to convey gentle sadness.

'LA GRECE ET LA SICILE'

The nineteenth century brought a renewed vision of ancient
Greece through the excavations and discoveries of archaeologists
and the study of its philosophies and religions. The stereotyped
ideas concerning antiquity shown by French art and poetry in
the seventeenth and eighteenth centuries gave way to a more
complex awareness of the life and thought of the Ancients. By
aptitude and training, Heredia was well equipped to indulge his
interest in Greek civilization.[6] It was the erudite Hellenist Louis
Ménard to whom Heredia and his master Leconte de Lisle owed
much for their knowledge of Greece. Heredia recounted with
gratitude how he received lessons from Ménard which, strength-
ened by the knowledge transmitted by Ménard through Leconte
de Lisle, gave him 'la compréhension générale, l'amour et le
regret de cette divine civilisation ensevelie sous les ruines des
temples' (Ibrovac, i, p. 243). Quite apart from such help and his
formal learning at school and university, Heredia's specifically
literary interests had already ensured his contact with Greece
through his love of Horace and Virgil and, nearer home, Ronsard
and Chénier, both of whom were admirers and imitators of
Greek literature.

The first three main subdivisions of 'La Grèce et la Sicile'—
'Hercule et les centaures', 'Artémis et les nymphes', 'Persée et
Andromède'—evoke various scenes from Greek legend and
mythology. Many of them—witness the horrible struggle of
'Centaures et Lapithes' or the bloodbath in 'Artémis'—are
striking for their colourful violence and barbarity. By their
panoramic, pictorial intensity they are partly a verbal anticipa-
tion of certain spectacular productions of twentieth-century

technicolor cinema—'la cinématographie poétique', as Fernand Brodel described them with some disdain in 1920.[7] They remind us of the novelist Flaubert, whose taste and talent bore some resemblance to Heredia's. Both had fundamentally 'romantic' temperaments: Heredia revelled in gorgeous, heroic visions of antiquity or of the Spanish *conquistadores* as Flaubert delighted in the luxuriant exoticism of the East (in his travels or in a novel like *Salammbô*). But both cherished and exemplified an ideal of impersonal art and both took great pains over their documentation, showing precise knowledge of the scenes they painted. Both embody a dichotomy calculated to interest psychoanalysts and irritate twentieth-century supporters of *la littérature engagée*: fairly conventional, bourgeois ways of living with no overt commitment to the contemporary society that bores or disgusts them and exultation through the imagination in the multicoloured and often barbaric splendours of the past. It would be reasonable if simplistic to argue that the relationship is causal, that the more ordered, disappointingly colourless and dull society is, the more alluring, in imagination and aesthetically distanced, violence and savagery can become. Once he feels at home amid the mythological scenery, the modern reader can undoubtedly derive great enjoyment from these exceptionally grandiose poems, which contribute as much as any to the high artistic standards of 'La Grèce et la Sicile'.

But these sonnets are not great because they exude exotic gore. Heredia's art is more complex than it often appears at first sight. The ferocity to which I have referred is only part of a broader context of vibrant sensuality expressed not just in the slaughter wrought by Artemis or Hercules but in the mounting eroticism of the Ariadne who 'rit au baiser prochain du Dompteur de l'Asie' and in the partly sadistic implications of the picture of Andromeda who, tied on her rock,

> Se lamente en tordant avec de vains sanglots
> Sa chair royale où court un frisson d'épouvante.

The beautiful heroine struggling helplessly as the train approaches on the railway track where she has been tied by the villain in early silent films like *The Perils of Pauline* can be seen as a less subtle descendant of Heredia's Andromeda (he uses the close-up —here, of the shivering flesh—more than the early cinema was

able to do). The centaur Nessus illustrates a curious blend of the
asexual open-air life that is still perhaps the glory of some rugby-
playing boarding-school adolescents (some of them take cold
showers like Nessus), bestial lust and nascent spiritual love. And
this very sensuality in which Heredia excels in 'La Grèce et la
Sicile' needs to be set in a still broader context, that of the in-
tensity and dramatic immediacy he constantly seeks in so many
ways.

There is some truth in Eugène Langevin's claim[8] that the
seeds of nearly all the section 'La Grèce et la Sicile' are to be
found in Théodore de Banville's *Les Stalactites* (1846), *Le Sang de
la coupe* (1857) and *Les Exilés* (1865) as well as in Leconte de
Lisle's *Poèmes antiques* (1852). Heredia's art is such that he is able
to make something distinctly original of material to some extent
common to him, Banville and Leconte de Lisle. But in fact, it was
mainly in his early years that Heredia was influenced by Banville,
in sonnets like 'Pan', 'Ariane', 'Artémis' or 'La Chasse' where his
themes are the same: Bacchus and Ariadne, Pan, the Satyrs, the
Nymphs and Bacchants. Banville provided Heredia with some
picturesque details, the elements of a good physical description.
It is claimed by other critics[9] that Heredia's later Greek sonnets
—those mostly published after the middle of the 1870s—are
much more ambitious, that they express the meaning of the
mythological figures involved. Some instances will clarify their
claims. Brunetière had asserted that Heredia's main concern in
the sonnet 'Andromède au monstre' was 'la beauté parfaite de
l'exécution';[10] though an allegorical meaning was doubtless to be
found once the poem had been composed, Heredia wrote it 'en
sculpteur et en peintre'. Joseph Vianey[11] disagreed, affirming that
Heredia definitely intended to show the primitive meaning of the
myth which he had found in Decharme's *La Mythologie grecque*
(1879). Perseus, like Hercules, Bellepheron and Oedipus, repre-
sented a solar god. Such myths embodied an episode in nature.
Pegasus represented the thunder while the monster itself was a
personification of the storm. In 'Stymphale', Hercules, for Here-
dia and mythologists of his time, represented the restorer of fine
weather, that is, the sun or purifying air. All the monsters de-
feated by Hercules were storm demons. Thousands of birds are
depicted in 'Stymphale' as rising from the lake 'ainsi qu'une
brusque rafale'. By this image Heredia is said to invert the per-

ception of primitive people for whom the dissipation of the storm was like the rising of countless birds. Heredia, Vianey claims, develops the two images so that they interpenetrate. Popular imagination had done the same, hence the birth of the myth: the victory of the sun over the clouds became the victory of the archer Hercules over the birds.

The somewhat ponderous academic approach of a Vianey can, by contrast, help us to appreciate the subtlety and discretion of Heredia's own erudition, which fuses so well with his delight in handling words and his love of mythology and art. Heredia would certainly have known of the meanings attributed to such myths. That he intended actually to show them in his poems as Vianey claims is contestable; rather, such knowledge is a background scarcely visible and surely not explicit in the sonnets. Other ramifications of this solar myth given by Vianey are even more contestable: 'la salle immense' in 'Centaures et Lapithes' is the counterpart of the sky; the Centaurs are called 'fils de la Nuée' and these equivalents of clouds have *black* breast-pieces and hair that *burns* in the reflections of the *torches*: 'ce sont des termes qui font songer aux ténèbres de l'orage traversées par les feux de l'éclair'. As for the noises brought by the Centaurs—cf. their feet, the table that is overturned, their shouts—'ce sont des bruits qui rappellent ceux de la tempête. Entre tant de traits qui pouvaient être pris pour peindre Hercule et les Centaures, le poète en a donc choisi qui fussent capables de faire reconnaître, chez ceux-ci, les démons de l'orage et, chez celui-ci, le soleil victorieux'.[12] With the single-minded zeal that characterized some nineteenth-century scholars, Vianey shows little awareness that other glosses may oust his. It is in any case certain that, for many readers, especially in our time, such interpretation is otiose. The poems are not made more enjoyable, their worth is not increased, by being so regarded.

In other interpretations, critics like Vianey and Ibrovac seem to be on sounder ground. Decisive points in man's evolution are recorded by Heredia: the defeat and destruction of local civilizations ('Marsyas'); the beginnings of man's finer instincts in creatures that still remain animals, symbols of prehistoric man ('Nessus', 'La Centauresse'). Such viewpoints are relevant, if fairly obvious, and they seem to form part of the contextual awareness of the poems in question.

The contributions of scholars have been perhaps of most use in the understanding of the fourth and last subsection of 'La Grèce et la Sicile'—'Epigrammes et Bucoliques', whose tone is much quieter and more elegiac than in the earlier parts. Indeed, the contrast with those earlier parts is very strong and we meet with our first evidence of the variety to be found in *Les Trophées*. Heredia evokes scenes from the everyday life of ancient Greece, still bathed in legends, still recalling nymphs, gods and godesses. But he is here concerned less with the great gods than the secondary ones, less with the outstandingly famous figures in history (found, for instance, in 'Rome et les Barbares') than with the life of the shepherd, the goatherd, the slave who longs to return to his native Sicily, the dignified ploughman bowed down with years, the young woman who has died on her wedding day. The characteristic note is sad, tender and soothing. It is a pastoral Greece we find here. Death is very present in this subsection, but not violent, glorious death. The predominant mood is of resigned regret that things pass away, including human life, amid the beauty of the natural world.

'Epigrammes et Bucoliques' show above all the influence of the Greek Anthology, which made itself felt in Heredia's published sonnets from 1888 (when the first five of 'Epigrammes et Bucoliques' appeared in *La Revue des deux mondes*). The first French translation of this anthology and its epigrams had appeared in two volumes in 1863.[13] The Greek Anthology had been read, loved and put to good poetic use by Ronsard and Du Bellay and also by Chénier in his elegies and idylls. The term 'epigram' had a wider sense for its Greek authors than it has for us now. Originally, it signified a simple inscription to perpetuate the memory of some deed or consecration. Then it was used to decorate the images of heroes; it was engraved on tombs or on trophies; it was sent with presents to a friend or mistress. It eventually celebrated stronger and wider themes, like the love of freedom and the hatred of tyrants. Few subjects failed to find their way into such epigrams—thus Anacreon used the form to sing of love and wine, Archilochos for stinging satire.[14] The Greek Anthology provided epigrams of many kinds: erotic, votive, funeral, descriptive, moral or exhortatory and comic. In the present subsection of 'La Grèce et la Sicile' we can note three main types used by Heredia. Firstly, there are votive epigrams like 'Les Bergers', 'Epigramme votive', 'Le Laboureur' and 'A Hermès Criophore'. In the Greek Anthology, a votive epigram is a short poem accompanying some offering to a god; a soldier would offer his shield, a cook his spit, a hunter his nets. The four sonnets mentioned give such precise instances, found by Heredia in the Greek Anthology. The name of a second type—funeral epigrams—is self-explanatory. 'La Prière du mort' owes much to the Greek Anthology. It mentions two kinds of death which illustrate the dangers of travel on land: murder and being devoured by wolves. 'Le Naufragé' is constructed on a basis of epigrams concerning another obvious kind of death the Greeks could encounter, drowning while making a sea journey. Thirdly, there is the descriptive epigram like 'Le Coureur' and 'Le Cocher', relating to epigrams concerning sports to be found in Greek sculpture as much as in the Greek Anthology.

Heredia's source was first pointed out, in 1910, by Emile Zilliacus.[15] Until then, his epigrammatic sonnets had been thought to be reminiscences of Greek art, e.g. a statue, a vase, a bas-relief. The strictly literary influence of the Greek Anthology seems here the more important. Zilliacus cogently notes the affinities between the Greek epigram and Heredia's type of sonnet: both are the ideal framework for poetry that is brief and dense, both provide a form well suited to the concentrated expression of a feeling or impression, both present firmness and clarity of outline and both tend to finish on a conceit or *pointe*. But it would be quite erroneous to imagine that Heredia was a mere slavish copier of the Greek Anthology. His use of it was similar to his use of his poetic predecessors of the nineteenth century, that is, it was an influence born of loving acquaintance and respect for the past. He is rarely satisfied with a mere translation. His treatment is free and sensitive. He will very often incorporate elements from several epigrams in one sonnet, leaving out what does not suit his poetic purpose. The Greek epigrams are often less a source for imitation than a vague model for exploitation. Thus 'La Jeune Morte' is inspired by many different epigrams about a young woman dying on her wedding day; Heredia generalizes much further this theme from the Greek Anthology, suggesting the sweetness of life and the horror of death for such a person, giving life and imagination to the often thin and arid language of the source. The young woman of his sonnet begs that the dove should

not be sacrificed on her tomb—'La vie est si douce, ah! laisse-la
vivre, ami'; not one of the many Greek epigrams on this theme
contains such a tender reflection and supplication. Very often,
too, Heredia uses his model as a point of departure for consider-
able originality of image, feeling or viewpoint. The quatrains of
'Le Laboureur' follow fairly closely a votive epigram in the Greek
Anthology but the *pointe* of the second tercet—the resonantly
suggestive depiction of the broken old peasant's fear of having to
continue his labours beyond death—is entirely Heredia's.

It seems that he took regular pleasure in reading the French
translation by Fr. Jacobs published by Hachette in 1863, as well
as the original Greek of the Anthology. The last word of the
French translation of an epigram is often the final word in
Heredia's sonnet (e.g. 'Epigramme funéraire', 'Le Naufragé', 'A
Hermès Criophore'). He sometimes uses words and phrases from
the French translation though other words and phrases would
have been closer to the Greek text.

'ROME ET LES BARBARES'

There are twenty-three sonnets in this section, compared with the
thirty-nine of 'La Grèce et la Sicile'. The numbers partly indicate
Heredia's instinctive preference. For him as for Leconte de Lisle
and Louis Ménard, ancient Greece was the true source of beauty
and goodness. Rome represented a decline. The coupling in the
same title of Rome and the Barbarians helps to create this im-
pression. Nearly all the pieces in 'Rome et les Barbares' appeared
late in Heredia's life, the majority, twelve, in the 1890s and all
but six after 1884. The last in the section, the three on Anthony
and Cleopatra and the epigraphic sonnets, were published before
the others. Does the relatively late composition of so many son-
nets here reflect Heredia's desire to give the section more body
and the whole collection better proportions? If his best love went
to Greece, he knew and cherished his Latin authors well enough
to find in them—e.g. Virgil, Horace, Juvenal, Livy, Plutarch,
Martial—what sources he needed for the present section. It has
been claimed that Heredia's style in various sonnets recalls the
individual manner of such Latin writers: the symmetry of Horace,
the condensed vigour of Propertius, the sonorously heroic pride
of Lucan, the ingenious artificiality of elocution in Martial.[16]

The section begins with four sonnets to various people and aspects of Rome in its greatness: the first to Virgil, the second to the Emperor Gallus who has retired to the country in the best fashion of wise Roman emperors, the third to the charms of the flute in the Italian countryside, the last to Sestius. There are sombre undertones in 'A Sextius' but the predominant spirit of the four sonnets is sober contentment, relish for the simple, good things that life can offer.

The next subdivision contains five poems concerning the 'God of the Gardens', that is, Priapus, son of Demeter and Aphrodite, personification of the idea of property. This Greek god once occupied a place of honour as a figurehead on the prows of ships. Later, he came to embody vegetable and animal fecundity and, as such, was honoured by herdsmen. The god Priapus's decline is illustrated by his final function for the Romans, that of scarecrow, protector of gardens and their produce. He was made fun of in popular stories. Sacrifices were offered to him as the god of orchards and gardens, especially in the countryside. The scarecrow was erected on a base, had billy-goat's horns and nanny-goat's ears, an obscene laugh on its face and held a club under its arm. The idea of using the figure of Priapus undoubtedly comes from the Latin poets, especially Catullus,[17] but some details are borrowed from the Greek Anthology and also the Latin Anthology.[18]

Artistically speaking, it is the dramatic presentation which enlivens this small subsection, dramatic because the god addresses his audience with forceful directness and because the five sonnets are a little drama in themselves as they depict the decline of Priapus, contrasting the dignity and honour he knew in the past with his now lowly status. There is also present, particularly in the third sonnet, a tone we have not encountered before in *Les Trophées*: grumbling, indulgent humour, a comic element heightened by the brisk, no-nonsense, conversational approach of the god of the gardens to the small boys out to steal from the farmer's garden.

'Rome et les Barbares' follows the procedure of 'La Grèce et la Sicile': it gives a selection of defining moments or scenes of a past civilization. There is both diversity and breadth of subject in the present subsection and we have further proof of the real if limited variety of *Les Trophées* and of Heredia's versatility; he does not confine himself to grandiose or brutal pictures nor to a tender, elegiac style. His knowledge nourishes his treatment, but unobtrusively. René Pichon praises the five sonnets of 'Hortorum Deus' for their portrayal of 'la vie familière, rustique et humble, des petites gens des faubourgs ou de la campagne'.[19] He singles out 'Villula', the second sonnet of 'Rome et les Barbares', for showing not just the externals of life in that time but two basic traits of the Romans, their moderation and their faithfulness to tradition. Ibrovac claims that the life and style of the Roman farmers are well suggested by 'Hortorum Deus': their attachment to the earth and their harsh egoism, so different from the gentleness and generosity to be found in many of the Greek sonnets (Ibrovac, i, p. 293). Here and later in 'Rome et les Barbares', something of the hardness and practical genius of the Romans is implied by Heredia's emphasis. The poems that follow offer still more themes and interests: in 'Le Tepidarium', the luxury and voluptuousness of the refined classes in their steam-baths; in 'La Trebbia' and 'Après Cannes', historical moments from the second Punic War, when Hannibal brought panic to the Romans; in the tryptych devoted to Anthony and Cleopatra, critical episodes in the history of Rome as its destiny begins to change with defeat and internal dissension. Pichon praises all these poems for their rare combination of technical precision regarding material details and the understanding they reveal of what was fundamental about the people and civilization in question. The three Cleopatra sonnets, like 'La Trebbia' and 'Après Cannes', are marvels of dramatic construction, beautiful for their firmness of outline and magic of sound, but, Pichon argues, they are not just decorative panels, for they show the old Roman soul succumbing to the perfidious indolence of Asia. Heredia avoids the danger of depicting vague, conventional abstractions—such as the essential Roman who figured in seventeenth-century French literature—yet his exact details about manners, furniture and institutions are far from being a lifeless display of erudition since they help to create portraits that are historically significant, psychologically human and artistically alive.

The inspiration of the last five sonnets, 'Sonnets épigraphiques', is perhaps the most recondite in the section. They are epigraphic because they are counterparts to the inscriptions on tombs found by archaeologists. Heredia himself explained how he came to write them.[20] He had relatives living near the Pyrenees and spent holidays with them as a young boy. In later life he went to Bagnères-de-Luchon to take the waters in 1874, 1880 and 1882, and it was there that the idea of the epigraphic sonnets was formed. Bored one day in his hotel, Heredia casually picked up from a table a book that had recently appeared, *Epigraphies de Luchon*, in which Julien Sacaze related the movements of a votive altar dedicated to the god Ilixon by Fabia Festa. Heredia's interest in Roman history was freshly aroused and also in a new group of *barbares*, the Gauls near Luchon who were conquered by the Romans. Under the Gauls, Luchon belonged to the area inhabited by the Garumni, formed of two races, Celtic and Spanish. From the second to the fifth centuries A.D., this region presented a strange mixture of barbarian and Roman culture. Graeco-Roman deities mingled with indigenous religions or superstitions, largely druidic, in a manner calculated to fascinate Parnassians like Heredia and Leconte de Lisle.[21] After the Roman conquest, local deities were adopted, globally described as *lares augustes* and existed comfortably with their Roman equivalents. The area abounded in votive altars to local gods and goddesses, hence the two mentioned in the ninth line of 'Le Vœu', Iscitt and Ilixon. The first was a pre-Roman god apparently corresponding to the Roman Vulcan, forger of metals, while the second was another pre-Roman barbarian god of the springs found in the district. It was local gods that the Gauls worshipped, those of springs, forests and mountains. In 'Le Vœu', Heredia gives a brief picture of these historical times, indicating how the Romans came to build their swimming-pools and hot baths. He has studied epigraphs or inscriptions and, like the barbarians of the district and the Romans later, he wishes to put up an altar, in verse, to the goddesses of the springs:

> . . . je veux
> Dresser l'autel barbare aux Nymphes Souterraines.

Here as elsewhere in *Les Trophées*—and most pointedly in 'La Source'—Heredia is drawn by the links between his own time and the past, by the manner in which past civilizations, though apparently gone for ever, still survive, if mainly in memory, and take on significance amid the natural scene and the life of modern man.

The appeal of these last five sonnets is perhaps less strong than that of many others found before this point in *Les Trophées*. Their themes are less universally known or important, they are less dramatic and, as in 'Le Vœu', the name-dropping may sometimes appear a too obtrusive substitute for the more appealing images and concrete evocations elsewhere. If such opinions have some justification, they are harsh in view of the sonnets' originality.

'LE MOYEN AGE ET LA RENAISSANCE'

The seventeen sonnets of the first subsection here are the most erudite and recondite in *Les Trophées*. Some readers unfamiliar with their themes will perhaps think them over-studied and overstrained. But it would be a total misconception to regard them as mere bookish lucubrations. On the contrary, several of them show how history and art, early passions for the young Heredia, came gloriously alive for him when, shortly after attaining his majority, he visited Italy with his friend Georges Lafenestre. The letters he wrote home to his mother during this tour of Italy's medieval and Renaissance treasures (first published in Ibrovac, i, pp. 251–73) are full of animated, sensitive and witty descriptions of all he saw in Milan, Verona, Venice, Padua, Genoa, Pisa, Florence or Leghorn. His intelligence, sensibility and aesthetic sense feasted on the riches Italy had to offer. An assiduous notetaker, he visited churches, museums and art galleries in the cities mentioned, copied inscriptions and bought stereoscopic pictures so that he and his mother at home could study at leisure what had attracted him. During the time not so employed, he went to the theatre or studied Italian and the history of painting. The descriptions of the paintings he sent home—Titian, Veronese, Giorgione, Cagliari, Giotto, Orcagna—or of the statues by such masters as Benvenuto Cellini showed that his responses could be strongly favourable or unfavourable and that he was no respecter of established reputations or received opinions. Raphael's *Marriage of the Virgin* left him 'parfaitement froid'; before Veronese's *Last Supper* he experienced 'une des plus grandes impressions qu'il soit donné à une âme d'artiste de ressentir'.

As might be expected, Heredia the tourist was not slow to generalize about the treasures he saw, to experience admiration and awe for the selflessness and devotion to their art of the Renaissance masters and to set them in a historical perspective which lay behind 'Le Moyen Age et la Renaissance' and all of *Les Trophées*. His attitude was characteristically amoral and aesthetic. We recognize in the following passage, from a letter, the historian and art-lover who was excited by the archaeological finds—in Greece or Luchon—that embodied pre-Christian or part Christian, part barbarian, values:

> Paganisme et christianisme s'amalgament singulièrement dans ce pays très chrétien, où tous les caprices de l'imagination, même la plus effrénée, étaient autorisés, pourvu que ce fût de l'art. C'est tout simplement fort immoral, mais en même temps si naïf que l'on n'a pas le courage de condamner les fantaisies de ces grands tailleurs de pierre ou de ces infatigables ouvriers de pinceau qui couvraient des kilomètres de murailles (sans exagération) et bâtissaient des monuments gigantesques en oubliant la plupart du temps de signer leur œuvre (quoted in Ibrovac, i, p. 254).

His stay in Verona brought the conclusion: 'Le Moyen Age, sanglant, superbe et grandiose, y vit tout entier par ses monuments'. The three adjectives underline the energy, colour and exotic barbarity to which Heredia was drawn and which he emphasizes in much of his poetry. But, as we have seen, there are other tones in his work; the grave though artistically pleasurable sadness which accompanies the realization that man's splendid creations pass away—the very first sonnet of *Les Trophées* introduced this perspective—is as present for him in Verona as it will be in the evocations of 'Les Conquérants': 'On s'attache singulièrement à ces villes tombées d'un passé glorieux dans une vie pire que la mort.'

    The tour of Italy with Lafenestre took place in 1864. There had been one earlier visit in 1861, a walking tour with two young friends. Heredia was to return there on his honeymoon in 1867. Though some of the sonnets in 'Le Moyen Age et la Renaissance' were first published fairly early in his career—'La Dogaresse' in 1867, 'A Claudius Popelin' in 1868—most belong to a later period. Heredia certainly kept alive his memories of what he saw in Italy but this section of *Les Trophées* is far from having those visits as its only source of inspiration. Several sonnets—'Vitrail', 'Epiphanie', 'Suivant Pétrarque', 'Sur le Livre des Amours de Pierre de Ronsard', 'La Belle Viole', 'Epitaphe' and 'Vélin doré'

—found their origin in literary reminiscence or in the splendours of medieval France. Heredia's own city, Paris, offered its art galleries and *objets d'art* and not just public collections. Most of the sonnets in this section are best looked at individually in the commentaries. It will be seen how associated Heredia was with certain key figures in the world of art in Paris: Claudius Popelin, painter, restorer and theorist of the *vieux arts du feu* and of the enamelling which provides the theme for 'Email' and 'Rêves d'émail'; the erudite Charles Davillier, fastidious collector of *objets d'art* from the Renaissance and other periods, to whom Heredia owed his inspiration and certain details in 'Le Vieil Orfèvre' and 'L'Estoc'; Charles Yriarte and Edouard de Beaumont with whom Heredia shared his enthusiasm for armorial bearings and swords; Edmond Bonnaffé whose scholarly devotion to the study of period furniture is reflected in 'Le Huchier de Nazareth' and 'Le Lit'. However removed they may seem from the usual run of our contemporary preoccupations—and Heredia was never 'popular' in his own day—and when due allowance has been made for the deliberate exploitation the art of poetry always was for him, all the sonnets in this section give sincere expression to authentic interests that absorbed Heredia and many of his friends. Some of these sonnets are among the purest and best *transpositions d'art* produced in the nineteenth century.

'Les Conquérants' concern the *conquistadores* who discovered and first began to develop the New World. No theme in *Les Trophées* was nearer Heredia's heart. Of Spanish blood through his father, he was born in Cuba and lived there during his early childhood. He was the descendant of Don Pedro de Heredia, El Adelantado, who took part in the expedition to the Indies of Bartholomew Columbus, brother of Christopher. The last four sonnets are devoted to this famous ancestor. The first sonnet, 'Les Conquérants', opens the subsection with a general evocation of the proud, adventurous and heroic figures who first set out to discover new lands across the Atlantic. 'Jouvence', 'Le Tombeau du Conquérant' and 'Carolo Quinto imperante' are dedicated to individual *conquistadores*. The subsection thus has a simple, strong unity. The *conquistadores* were literally in Heredia's blood, but the sonnets are not just the celebration of family pride; he was drawn to the spirit represented by the adventurers, to the boldness of their projects and the colourful intensity of their experiences.

Heredia's deeply personal interest in the conquest of the New World led him to read much of what had been written on the subject. His library contained 185 volumes on America. The first sonnet of the subsection was also the first to be composed and published, in 1868. In 1869, he published his 'Conquérants de l'or', which was intended as the prologue to a long epic poem about the conquest of Peru and the fortunes of the Indians. The poem was never written. But Heredia devoted some fifteen years to a labour of love, the translation from the Spanish of the *Historia Verdadera de la Conquista de la Nueva España* (1630) by Bernal Díaz. (See my *Heredia*, Athlone French Poets, pp. 71–81.) The four long tomes of this prose translation appeared in 1877, 1879, 1881 and 1887 and were widely acknowledged as a masterpiece of erudition and subtle artistry. The remaining sonnets of 'Les Conquérants' give therefore only a glimpse of the vaster ambitions Heredia entertained for the exploitation of his theme and of the comprehensive knowledge he acquired concerning it. It is a kind of poetic justice that the attention he gave to Latin America has been repaid by the considerable following he continues to enjoy there. We may, for example, note that the translations into Spanish of *Les Trophées* in the two annotated editions given in our Bibliography were published in Buenos Aires and Mexico.

'L'ORIENT ET LES TROPIQUES'

Anyone speaking of Heredia runs the risk of overworking the word 'exotic'. It is certainly one of the most appropriate to describe his sonnets. But they reveal different kinds of exoticism. In 'Le Moyen Age et la Renaissance', it is fairly unusual and recondite, whereas in 'L'Orient et les tropiques' it is more accessible for the majority of readers and, in the context of nineteenth-century French poetry, more conventional. Unlike some writers such as Gautier and Flaubert, Heredia did not travel far away from France (though he had come from Cuba); Italy and Spain were the only foreign countries he visited. For him, knowledge fired by imagination replaced travel. His acquaintance with the countries which, however briefly, are in some way evoked in 'L'Orient et les tropiques'—Egypt, Japan, South America with its Andes in 'Fleurs de feu' and 'Fleur séculaire'—was formed

from various sources. As we have seen in respect of 'Les Con-
quérants', his habitual wide reading was an important one.[22] His
interest in *objets d'art* was another. He shared with friends like
Edmond de Goncourt or the art critic Louis Gonse the pastime of
hunting down Eastern curios and trinkets. 'Le Samouraï' (1884)
and 'Le Daïmio' (1893) came late in Heredia's career and were
one manifestation of the fashion for things Japanese that was
stimulated by the universal exhibition in 1878. He knew many of
the most erudite *japonisants* of his time, like Bing, Gillet, Hayashi
and Montefiore. He was able to loan thirty-nine of his own pieces
to the retrospective exhibition of Japanese art which was organ-
ized in 1883 exclusively from private collections. In this section of
Les Trophées as in others, we encounter some of the fruit of Here-
dia's erudition and also of his devotion to art.

But the biggest single source of these sonnets is undoubtedly
previous literature. The earliest, 'Fleurs de feu' (1866), and also
'Fleur séculaire' (1876) owe much to Banville and something to
Leconte de Lisle, though despite the common tendency to con-
sider the Andes as Leconte de Lisle's range of mountains—largely
through the much anthologized 'Le Sommeil du condor'—we
have seen that Heredia made South America one of his own liter-
ary domains. The first three sonnets (1874) form a short Egyptian
cycle. The Middle East was more exotic then than now. Now we
commonly regard it as a source of oil and an arid political 'trouble-
spot' which could plunge the world into a third global war; then
it was relatively mysterious and on that account bewitched the
imagination. Heredia's sonnets about Egypt were written when
the discoveries of archaeologists like Mariette were opening up
new knowledge of its past civilizations. Gautier, Leconte de Lisle
and Léon Dierx were the most important influences of a strictly
literary nature lying behind 'La Vision de Khèm'. The theme of
Egypt in nineteenth-century French literature originated from
the enthusiasm engendered by the discovery of the Pyramids and
of that country's culture at the time of Napoleon's Nile campaign
(1798–9). This campaign resulted in the founding of Egyptology
and the vogue for things Egyptian in furniture, art and literature.
Of the three poets just mentioned, Gautier is by far the most
important, with his tale *Une Nuit de Cléopâtre* (1845) and his novel
Le Roman de la momie (1858). If Heredia's Egyptian sonnets are
better than those poems of Gautier, Leconte de Lisle or Léon

Dierx which are based on similar themes, it is because of their dramatic density and concentration. The harshness and inhumanity of his selected scenes are intensified to a point of vibrant exultation as he vividly recreates the hierarchical rigidity and bigotry of past Egyptian cultures. The original title when they were first published in 1874 was 'La Terre de Khèmi', which included three other sonnets not taken up in *Les Trophées*. One depicted dawn on the river Nile, with the mention of gazelles, another evoked evening falling over the same scene as the Egyptian women, the *fellaheen*, bearing their jars, walk laughing down to the river for water and the third involved a similar twilight scene with a Nubian buffalo stamping heavily into a rice-swamp. They are good poems and their exclusion from *Les Trophées* illustrates Heredia's art of sacrifice. 'La Vision de Khèm' is more concentratedly forceful for being no more than a triptych, and the tone of harsh inhumanity is heightened by thus removing all traces of anything living, human (the *fellaheen*) or even animal (gazelle or buffalo).

If the sonnets of 'L'Orient et les tropiques' seem banal and too derivative for the understandably fastidious taste of those most informed about nineteenth-century French poetry, if 'Fleurs de feu' and 'Fleur séculaire' are too obviously and grandiloquently climactic, the density of the Egyptian sonnets to which I have referred, the imaginative bizarreness of a poem like 'Le Samouraï' or the superb combination of precision and suggestion exemplified by 'Le Récif de corail' ensure that this short section, while presenting a different appeal, does not fall below the high standard set by the longest section, 'La Grèce et la Sicile'.

'LA NATURE ET LE REVE'

The title of this last group of sonnets—probably inspired by the poet Armand Silvestre, an old friend of Heredia[23]—could scarcely be more comprehensive. Nature is present enough in the rest of *Les Trophées* and, it could be argued, we also find there much of the suggestion associated with the word *rêve*. Heredia clearly intended that his title here should imply something more explicitly personal—as in 'La Sieste', 'Brise marine' or 'Au Tragédien E. Rossi'—where the simple *je* is not afraid to appear. One is inevitably prompted to reflect that, in his poetry, Heredia observes the strictest self-imposed standards of reticence. Even in this section, there is no very revealing self-confession. But by contrast with all the other sections, some sonnets have not just a more obviously personal and even anecdotic basis but are concerned with life as it is lived in Heredia's own time, especially in the subsection 'La Mer de Bretagne', where 'nature' figures most largely, a nature very different from that of the hot tropics, Egypt or South America. Heredia went frequently to Brittany throughout his life and sometimes for long stays, particularly to Douarnenez in the west. He loved to walk there, was especially fond of the sea and also enjoyed in Brittany the company of good friends like the landscape artist Emmanuel Lansyer, to whom he dedicated, in 1887, his sonnet 'Arvor' (which later became 'Bretagne') and eventually, in *Les Trophées*, all the sonnets of 'La Mer de Bretagne'. It is Lansyer who is the painter of 'Un Peintre'. Like Heredia, he loved the bay of Douarnenez which he represented in his works in many states and at different hours of the day, so much so that it is difficult to be sure how much Heredia's Breton poems owe to his own lived experience and how much to his fondness for Lansyer's paintings. Like Lansyer, Heredia specializes in the west coast of the Finistère peninsula; only one poem, 'Maris Stella', depicts its north coast, at Roscoff, and then much less the sea than the scene on the shore. Yet again, we can appreciate the interpenetration of painting and poetry in Heredia's life and art. If he, the *paysagiste en mots*, was influenced by Lansyer, Lansyer himself composed sonnets to accompany his canvases.[24]

'La Mer de Bretagne' contains the best in this section. A sonnet like 'Maris Stella' evokes the hard life of the fishermen and their wives. The classical commonplace 'Que de hardis pêcheurs qui ne reviendront pas!' touches on their suffering but in a perspective that is predominantly artistic, from a viewpoint that savours the sombre beauty of this forlorn scene of eternal human endurance beneath the washed skies of Brittany tinged with sunset hues. Not only is there no detailed self-confession in 'La Nature et le rêve' but what is personal is presented fairly impersonally or in various ways universalized. The lover of pure beauty or the verbal painter is very much in evidence in poems like 'Floridum Mare' or 'Soleil couchant', while 'Blason céleste' is a poetic purple passage showing Heredia's sophisticatedly conscious artistry as he develops the relationship between heraldry and sunset. As always, he is drawn to the past that survives, the crumbling manors in 'Un Peintre' or the menhirs in 'Bretagne'. The eternal comes to the fore in statuesque and general terms as he evokes 'L'homme immuable auprès de l'immuable chose' ('Bretagne'). The present scene is firmly if discreetly linked to the gods and the mythology of past civilizations when for him

> . . . la même clameur que pousse encor la mer
> Monte de l'homme aux Dieux, vainement éternelle

or when the stallion with its rider entering the sea recalls, in the first line of 'Le Bain', the centaur of 'La Grèce et la Sicile'. And in 'Le Bain' the tone of 'Nessus' is not far away, for here as in 'La Grèce et la Sicile', Heredia is attracted to the dramatically grandiose and energetic as, stallion and rider,

> Ils opposent, cabrés, leur poitrail noir qui fume,
> Au fouet échevelé de la fumante écume.

Violent, stormy seas, as in 'Mer montante', strike an answering chord in Heredia, whose spirit, expressed through the imagery, grows tempestuous before it finally subsides with the equivalent of a musical cadence, with a sense of the universal in time's passage and a bitter, grave sadness made pleasurable by the power which both his perceptions and his art have to discern the significant and the beautiful.

The sonnets in 'La Mer de Bretagne' extend over all Heredia's career, from 1868 to 1892. Some of the others in 'La Nature et le rêve' are fairly early, like 'La Mort de l'aigle' (1864), 'La Conque' (1866) and 'Les Funérailles' (1868). The 'rêve' of the title, we have noted, implies the reverie inspired by nature but also the more personal note of some of the poems not connected with Brittany. Four of them, 'Médaille antique', 'Les Funérailles', 'Vendange' and 'Sur un marbre brisé' are really Grecian and seem to belong to the first section of *Les Trophées*; the first three in fact did, in publications before 1893. Their inspiration is hardly more personal than that of a subsection like 'Les Conquérants'. 'Le Lit' and 'Michel-Ange' would seem better placed in 'Le Moyen Age et la Renaissance'. The quality of the sonnets not inspired by Brittany seems to be less high than that of most in *Les Trophées*. Thus 'Le Lit' has a good central theme but too much plain enumeration and too many unexciting platitudes (it appeared in 1887 with 'Le Huchier de Nazareth', which is greatly superior for reasons examined in the commentary), while 'Au Tragédien E. Rossi' reveals Heredia's dramatic tendencies at their weakest: like 'La Mort de l'aigle', it appears too mechanically contrived and is perhaps too anecdotic to merit a place at all in *Les Trophées*. In brief, the sonnets in 'La Nature et le rêve' lie somewhat uneasily together and it is difficult to resist the impression that some find themselves in this section less for any positive reason than because Heredia felt they were not suitable for inclusion elsewhere in his collection.

THE ART OF 'LES TROPHEES'

Heredia's artistry is too large a subject to receive in the limited scope of this edition the full treatment it warrants. I have sought in the major part of my introduction to characterize the five main sections of his collection. His technique in *Les Trophées* calls for the detailed commentaries provided later. To appreciate his real if limited genius we need to see him not just in relation to his other works but also in the perspective of French poetry, at least that of his century. These requirements are met by the monograph in the Athlone French Poets series. The remaining pages of my introduction offer some brief conclusions and suggestions which the monograph explores more comprehensively.

No poet worthy of the name can be adequately understood or even described merely in terms of his subject-matter. Theme and form in poetry—and in much prose—are two facets of something which is really indivisible and which we separate only for the convenience of exposition and orderly comprehension. In the main part of *Les Trophées*, what we mostly mean by form is the structure called the sonnet. This is very much the verse-form of the keenly conscious and even self-conscious poet. I said at the beginning that Heredia is largely devoid of preoccupations with society, morality or contemporary issues or even with ideas as such, that he avoids personal confession and effusiveness. The indivisibility of *fond* and *forme* is firmly brought home to us if we realize that this earlier statement, regarding the *fond* of *Les Trophées*, is one way of giving expression to what is inherent in the very form of the sonnet, certainly as it is handled by Heredia.

A verse-form so short and relatively fixed is not only suitable to his style of writing, it *is* it. Implicit in his use of the sonnet is a certain attitude to language and poetry: he seeks to build his appeal on a deliberate exploitation of language that is meant, more than most poetry, to be enjoyed unhurriedly for its own sake. It seems no accident that the sonnet was not much used by those Romantic poets who, to take up Valéry's famous if crude distinction, were more concerned to *say* than to *make* or *do*. As the century progressed and poetry evolved partly in reaction against the effusiveness of the early Romantics, the sonnet enjoyed a great vogue. Masters like Nerval, Baudelaire and Mallarmé excelled in it.

This fixed form, already traditional and, so to speak, conservative by its nature, is used by Heredia in a manner that reinforces that nature. He keeps consistently to a number of rules or procedures. A few facts will illustrate the point. Firstly, rhyme-scheme: of 117 sonnets, 72 follow the pattern ABBA ABBA CCDEDE, 31 the pattern ABBA ABBA CCDEED. So the two patterns, those most frequently used before Heredia, account for 103 of the 117 sonnets. Every sonnet has *rimes embrassées* with different rhyming words in the two quatrains. The variations in the remaining 14 sonnets are found only in the sestets and all had been used before Heredia: 7 follow the pattern CDDCEE, 3 CDCDEE, 2 CDCDCD, 1 CDDCDC and 1 CCDDCD. Of these rhymes very nearly half are *riches*, a slightly smaller number are *suffisantes* while some 35 are *pauvres*; there are a couple of defective rhymes.[25] Throughout *Les Trophées*, without exception, Heredia uses the alexandrine. The punctuation too is worth a mention: all the sonnets have a full stop at the end of the first and second quatrains, with only three exceptions (which are semi-colons): at the end of line 11, 69 sonnets have a semi-colon, 41 have a full stop, 1 has a colon, 4 a comma, 1 a dash and 1 no punctuation at all. It would be dangerous to draw too sweeping conclusions from such considerations but they clearly help to illustrate that Heredia's sonnets have what the French call *tenue*: most of them are decorous, some are majestic and grandiloquent, their tone is often aristocratic, resolutely distant from the familiar or intimate. The sonnet is a fixed form but it does allow certain variations and, with regard to rhyme-schemes and length of lines, a degree of freedom from which a poet like Baudelaire was able to profit with excellent results. Heredia chooses on the whole not to use these possibilities. His self-imposed limitation may be thought to lead to a static quality in the sonnets. To some extent, it does, but the question is extremely complex: the features noted concerning verse-form, rhyme and punctuation tend rather to emphasize—indeed, partly to constitute—his sonorous use of language, but there is also between the dramatic dynamism of his images or rhythms and the restrictions of the sonnet structure a curious and often subtle tension which requires of the reader much thoughtful sensitivity. Between the fixed twelve syllables of the alexandrine and the subtle flexibility within the body of the line a similar relationship can be noted, created largely by variations of the *coupes* in a manner which recalls the masterly versification of a Racine.

Throughout *Les Trophées* we can see abundant evidence of the close connection between Heredia's poems and the visual arts, especially painting. It has been emphasized that his sonnets follow the nineteenth-century tradition of the *transposition d'art*, that their effect is to a considerable extent pictorial. But this way of seeing him runs the risk of distorting the truth: if it is useful to see links between some sonnets and some films in glorious technicolour, the comparison must not be pushed too far or it will quite neglect the non-visual, the intellectually verbal subtlety more inherent in a complex linguistic creation than in a fairly simple cinematographic one. The appeal of the flexible alexandrine's rhythms, the reader's constantly returning pleasure in the symmetry of rhyme, the euphony, harmony and often the subtle delight in controlled harshness or roughness of sound, all form an important part of Heredia's power of expression. The description and analysis of these factors can be difficult and full of dangers, especially of the wilder kinds of subjectivism, but the actual appreciation of them by the sensitive reader, in the context of all the rest of the poem, and in the time-scale imposed by the poem, vitally distinguishes these sonnets not just from other non-linguistic achievements but from other uses of language or other poets' compositions. What André Spire called 'l'effort buccal' that is required of the reader of poetry is particularly required of the reader of *Les Trophées*. To be fully relished, the sonnets need to be read aloud (at the least, with a good, articulating, 'internal' voice). They need to be tasted in the mouth, reflectively savoured.

'Dramatic dynamism' or 'dramatic immediacy' are phrases I have used in an attempt to refer comprehensively to a large range of effects which are the very stuff of *Les Trophées*. However pictorial Heredia's manner may be, a poem can never, like a painting, give an immediate synthesis: the verbal picture has to be built up and Heredia exploits the dynamic effect of the succession thus entailed. Octet and sestet are frequently contrasted; his art consists of setting up the characters and/or situation in the first quatrain or in the octet, while the sestet exploits them with a note often more sharply urgent, leading to a climax in the last line. It is a common claim, often meant pejoratively, that Heredia's first thirteen lines are written for the impact of the last, *le vers définitif*. There is obviously some truth in this: many sonnets end with lines that remain firmly in the memory because of their supremely climactic quality. But the view to which I have referred quite underestimates the dramatic effect to be found in the body of many sonnets—such as 'Soir de bataille', 'La Vision de Khèm' (I and II), 'Mer montante' or 'La Mort de l'aigle'. It also fails to take account of the variety of climaxes in the last line. Some are predominantly pictorial and violent: 'La gigantesque horreur de l'ombre Herculéenne' ('Fuite de Centaures') or 'Sur le ciel enflammé, l'Imperator sanglant' ('Soir de bataille'), but even in these, of course, sound and rhythm, as well as contrast, play an important role. The suggestion in other last lines is more restrainedly menacing, implying vistas that open up in the imagination: 'Le piétinement sourd des légions en marche' ('La Trebbia') or 'Toute une mer immense où fuyaient des galères' ('Antoine et Cléopâtre'). Others are very quietly climactic, like the delicately shimmering 'Les minarets pointus qui tremblent dans le Nil' ('Le Prisonnier').

The themes of some sonnets in *Les Trophées*—like 'Centaures et Lapithes' or 'Après Cannes'—are no doubt such that they would have been dramatic if handled by any competent poet. One doubts if they would have been so densely dramatic. Heredia knows how to vary his approach, sometimes addressing the reader directly, sometimes apostrophizing Nature, at other times letting the character in the sonnet speak directly himself: all these different uses of speech form an integral part of the sonnets' dramatic appeal. In the use of contrasting direct speech, 'Sphinx' is of course the most striking in the whole collection (though perhaps not very successful because Heredia has compressed so much into it, imparting a pace so hurried that it can appear too forced and confused). In respect of direct speech, 'L'Epée' is an interestingly successful example. It is a description of a sword, and could have run the risk of being too static or dull. By dwelling on the sword's basic inspiration, its potential appeal to martial feelings, by speaking directly himself, by introducing yet another character, a young boy, to whom is addressed a series of urgent imperatives, Heredia breathes life and movement into his poem. Those who love *Les Trophées* will be able to pursue further the ramifications of this dramatic immediacy, like his fondness for antithesis and contrast (of sense, or colour or sound) or for silhouettes set against backgrounds. His last lines usually stand out above all the others not just because they are led up to syntactically but because they constitute a greater controlled concentration of all the elements indicated, at their most intense expressed by an arresting fusion of opposites, by oxymoron, as in 'Silencieusement vers le soleil aboie' ('La Vision de Khèm I').

Among many poets who have admired *Les Trophées*, the young Paul Valéry was undoubtedly thinking of Heredia, as well as of others like Baudelaire and Mallarmé, when, with all the enthusiasm of his eighteen years, he set down in 1889 his conception of the poet's role: 'tout ce qu'il aura imaginé, senti, songé, échafaudé, passera au crible, sera pesé, épuré, mis à la *forme* et condensé le plus possible pour gagner en force ce qu'il sacrifie en longueur: un sonnet, par exemple, sera une véritable quintessence, un osmazôme, un suc concentré et cohobé, réduit à quatorze vers soigneusement *composé* en vue d'un effet final et foudroyant'.[26] Many of Heredia's sonnets carry a potentially explosive tension, some more obviously than others. Whether the theme and manner are apparently violent or gentle, nearly all *Les Trophées* strike home, involving the poet's and our powers of sensuous enjoyment through the sensitive exploitation of the infinite possibilities of language in a restricted but flexible framework.

At the request of the General Editor, I have not included two rather long poems, 'Romancero' and 'Les Conquérants de l'or', which followed the famous sonnet sequence in the 1893 volume. Both these poems are in the epic vein, the first in *terza rima* and the other in *rimes plates*, and they have rarely been considered as an integral part of *Les Trophées*. For all information concerning these two poems, the reader is referred to my monograph in this series.

LES
TROPHEES

par

JOSE-MARIA DE HEREDIA

L'amour sans plus du verd Laurier m'agrée.

PIERRE DE RONSARD

A PARIS

CHEZ ALPHONSE LEMERRE

1893

MANIBVS
CARISSIMAE
ET
AMANTISSIMAE
MATRIS
FILIVS MEMOR
J. M. H.

A LECONTE DE LISLE

C'est à vous, cher et illustre ami, que j'aurais dédié ces Trophées, si le respect d'une mémoire sacrée qui, je le sais, vous est chère aussi, ne m'eût interdit d'inscrire un nom, si glorieux soit-il, au frontispice de ce livre.

Un à un, vous les avez vus naître, ces poèmes. Ils sont comme des chaînons qui nous rattachent au temps déjà lointain où vous enseigniez aux jeunes poètes, avec les règles et les subtils secrets de notre art, l'amour de la poésie pure et du pur langage français. Je vous suis plus redevable que tout autre : vous m'avez jugé digne de l'honneur de votre amitié. J'ai pu, au cours d'une longue intimité, comprendre mieux l'excellence de vos préceptes et de vos conseils, la beauté de votre exemple. Et mon titre le plus sûr à quelque gloire, sera d'avoir été votre élève bien aimé.

C'est pour vous complaire que je recueille mes vers épars. Vous m'avez assuré que ce livre, bien qu'en partie inachevé, garderait néanmoins aux yeux du lecteur indulgent quelque chose de la noble ordonnance que j'avais rêvée. Tel qu'il est, je vous l'offre, non sans regret de n'avoir pu mieux faire, mais avec la conscience d'avoir fait de mon mieux.

Recevez-le, cher et illustre ami, en témoignage de mon affectueuse gratitude, et comme il serait malséant de clore sans le vœu traditionnel une épître liminaire, quelque brève qu'elle soit, permettez que je vous souhaite, à vous et à tous ceux qui feuilleteront ces pages, de prendre à lire ces poèmes autant de plaisir que j'eus à les composer.

JOSE-MARIA DE HEREDIA

LA GRECE ET LA SICILE

L'Oubli

Le temple est en ruine au haut du promontoire.
Et la Mort a mêlé, dans ce fauve terrain,
Les Déesses de marbre et les Héros d'airain
Dont l'herbe solitaire ensevelit la gloire.   4

Seul, parfois, un bouvier menant ses buffles boire,
De sa conque où soupire un antique refrain
Emplissant le ciel calme et l'horizon marin,
Sur l'azur infini dresse sa forme noire.   8

La Terre maternelle et douce aux anciens Dieux,
Fait à chaque printemps, vainement éloquente,
Au chapiteau brisé verdir une autre acanthe;

Mais l'Homme indifférent au rêve des aïeux   12
Écoute sans frémir, du fond des nuits sereines,
La Mer qui se lamente en pleurant les Sirènes.

HERCULE ET LES CENTAURES

Némée

Depuis que le Dompteur entra dans la forêt
En suivant sur le sol la formidable empreinte,
Seul, un rugissement a trahi leur étreinte.
Tout s'est tu. Le soleil s'abîme et disparaît.   4

A travers le hallier, la ronce et le guéret,
Le pâtre épouvanté qui s'enfuit vers Tirynthe
Se tourne, et voit d'un œil élargi par la crainte
Surgir au bord des bois le grand fauve en arrêt.   8

Il s'écrie. Il a vu la terreur de Némée
Qui sur le ciel sanglant ouvre sa gueule armée,
Et la crinière éparse et les sinistres crocs;

Car l'ombre grandissante avec le crépuscule   12
Fait, sous l'horrible peau qui flotte autour d'Hercule,
Mêlant l'homme à la bête, un monstrueux héros.

Stymphale

Et partout devant lui, par milliers, les oiseaux,
De la berge fangeuse où le Héros dévale,
S'envolèrent, ainsi qu'une brusque rafale,
Sur le lugubre lac dont clapotaient les eaux.   4

D'autres, d'un vol plus bas croisant leurs noirs réseaux,
Frôlaient le front baisé par les lèvres d'Omphale,
Quand, ajustant au nerf la flèche triomphale,
L'Archer superbe fit un pas dans les roseaux.   8

Et dès lors, du nuage effarouché qu'il crible,
Avec des cris stridents, plut une pluie horrible
Que l'éclair meurtrier rayait de traits de feu.

Enfin, le Soleil vit, à travers ces nuées   12
Où son arc avait fait d'éclatantes trouées,
Hercule tout sanglant sourire au grand ciel bleu.

Nessus

Du temps que je vivais à mes frères pareil
Et comme eux ignorant d'un sort meilleur ou pire,
Les monts Thessaliens étaient mon vague empire
Et leurs torrents glacés lavaient mon poil vermeil.   4

Tel j'ai grandi, beau, libre, heureux, sous le soleil;
Seule, éparse dans l'air que ma narine aspire,
La chaleureuse odeur des cavales d'Epire
Inquiétait parfois ma course ou mon sommeil.   8

Mais depuis que j'ai vu l'Epouse triomphale
Sourire entre les bras de l'Archer de Stymphale,
Le désir me harcèle et hérisse mes crins;

Car un Dieu, maudit soit le nom dont il se nomme!   12
A mêlé dans le sang enfiévré de mes reins
Au rut de l'étalon l'amour qui dompte l'homme.

La Centauresse

Jadis, à travers bois, rocs, torrents et vallons
Errait le fier troupeau des Centaures sans nombre;
Sur leurs flancs le soleil se jouait avec l'ombre,
Ils mêlaient leurs crins noirs parmi nos cheveux blonds.   4

L'été fleurit en vain l'herbe. Nous la foulons
Seules. L'antre est désert que la broussaille encombre;
Et parfois je me prends, dans la nuit chaude et sombre,
A frémir à l'appel lointain des étalons.   8

Car la race de jour en jour diminuée
Des fils prodigieux qu'engendra la Nuée,
Nous délaisse et poursuit la Femme éperdument.

C'est que leur amour même aux brutes nous ravale;   12
Le cri qu'il nous arrache est un hennissement,
Et leur désir en nous n'étreint que la cavale.

Centaures et Lapithes

La foule nuptiale au festin s'est ruée,
Centaures et guerriers ivres, hardis et beaux;
Et la chair héroïque, au reflet des flambeaux,
Se mêle au poil ardent des fils de la Nuée.   4

Rires, tumulte . . . Un cri! . . . L'Epouse polluée
Que presse un noir poitrail, sous la pourpre en lambeaux
Se débat, et l'airain sonne au choc des sabots
Et la table s'écroule à travers la huée.   8

Alors celui pour qui le plus grand est un nain,
Se lève. Sur son crâne, un mufle léonin
Se fronce, hérissé de crins d'or. C'est Hercule.

Et d'un bout de la salle immense à l'autre bout,   12
Dompté par l'œil terrible où la colère bout,
Le troupeau monstrueux en renâclant recule.

Fuite de Centaures

Ils fuient, ivres de meurtre et de rébellion,
Vers le mont escarpé qui garde leur retraite;
La peur les précipite, ils sentent la mort prête
Et flairent dans la nuit une odeur de lion.   4

Ils franchissent, foulant l'hydre et le stellion,
Ravins, torrents, halliers, sans que rien les arrête;
Et déjà, sur le ciel, se dresse au loin la crête
De l'Ossa, de l'Olympe ou du noir Pélion.   8

Parfois, l'un des fuyards de la farouche harde
Se cabre brusquement, se retourne, regarde,
Et rejoint d'un seul bond le fraternel bétail;

Car il a vu la lune éblouissante et pleine   12
Allonger derrière eux, suprême épouvantail,
La gigantesque horreur de l'ombre Herculéenne.

La Naissance d'Aphrodité

Avant tout, le Chaos enveloppait les mondes
Où roulaient sans mesure et l'Espace et le Temps;
Puis Gaia, favorable à ses fils les Titans,
Leur prêta son grand sein aux mamelles fécondes.   4

Ils tombèrent. Le Styx les couvrit de ses ondes.
Et jamais, sous l'éther foudroyé, le Printemps
N'avait fait resplendir les soleils éclatants,
Ni l'Eté généreux mûri les moissons blondes.   8

Farouches, ignorants des rires et des jeux,
Les Immortels siégeaient sur l'Olympe neigeux.
Mais le ciel fit pleuvoir la virile rosée;

L'Océan s'entr'ouvrit, et dans sa nudité   12
Radieuse, émergeant de l'écume embrasée,
Dans le sang d'Ouranos fleurit Aphrodité.

Jason et Médée

A Gustave Moreau

En un calme enchanté, sous l'ample frondaison
De la forêt, berceau des antiques alarmes,
Une aube merveilleuse avivait de ses larmes,
Autour d'eux, une étrange et riche floraison.   4

Par l'air magique où flotte un parfum de poison,
Sa parole semait la puissance des charmes;
Le Héros la suivait et sur ses belles armes
Secouait les éclairs de l'illustre Toison.   8

Illuminant les bois d'un vol de pierreries,
De grands oiseaux passaient sous les voûtes fleuries,
Et dans les lacs d'argent pleuvait l'azur des cieux.

L'Amour leur souriait, mais la fatale Epouse   12
Emportait avec elle et sa fureur jalouse
Et les philtres d'Asie et son père et les Dieux.

ARTEMIS ET LES NYMPHES

Artémis

L'âcre senteur des bois montant de toutes parts,
Chasseresse, a gonflé ta narine élargie,
Et dans ta virginale et virile énergie,
Rejetant tes cheveux en arrière, tu pars ! 4

Et du rugissement des rauques léopards
Jusqu'à la nuit tu fais retentir Ortygie,
Et bondis à travers la haletante orgie
Des grands chiens éventrés sur l'herbe rouge épars. 8

Et, bien plus, il te plaît, Déesse, que la ronce
Te morde et que la dent ou la griffe s'enfonce
Dans tes bras glorieux que le fer a vengés ;

Car ton cœur veut goûter cette douceur cruelle 12
De mêler, en tes jeux, une pourpre immortelle
Au sang horrible et noir des monstres égorgés.

La Chasse

Le quadrige, au galop de ses étalons blancs,
Monte au faîte du ciel, et les chaudes haleines
Ont fait onduler l'or bariolé des plaines.
La Terre sent la flamme immense ardre ses flancs.   4

La forêt masse en vain ses feuillages plus lents;
Le Soleil, à travers les cimes incertaines
Et l'ombre où rit le timbre argentin des fontaines,
Se glisse, darde et luit en jeux étincelants.   8

C'est l'heure flamboyante où, par la ronce et l'herbe,
Bondissant au milieu des molosses, superbe,
Dans les clameurs de mort, le sang et les abois,

Faisant voler les traits de la corde tendue,   12
Les cheveux dénoués, haletante, éperdue,
Invincible, Artémis épouvante les bois.

Nymphée

Le quadrige céleste à l'horizon descend,
Et, voyant fuir sous lui l'occidentale arène,
Le Dieu retient en vain de la quadruple rêne
Ses étalons cabrés dans l'or incandescent.   4

Le char plonge. La mer, de son soupir puissant,
Emplit le ciel sonore où la pourpre se traîne,
Tandis qu'à l'Est d'où vient la grande Nuit sereine
Silencieusement s'argente le Croissant.   8

Voici l'heure où la Nymphe, au bord des sources fraîches,
Jette l'arc détendu près du carquois sans flèches.
Tout se tait. Seul, un cerf brame au loin vers les eaux.

La lune tiède luit sur la nocturne danse,   12
Et Pan, ralentissant ou pressant la cadence,
Rit de voir son haleine animer les roseaux.

Pan

A travers les halliers, par les chemins secrets
Qui se perdent au fond des vertes avenues,
Le Chèvre-pied, divin chasseur de Nymphes nues,
Se glisse, l'œil ardent, sous les hautes forêts.   4

Il est doux d'écouter les soupirs, les bruits frais
Qui montent à midi des sources inconnues
Quand le Soleil, vainqueur étincelant des nues,
Dans la mouvante nuit darde l'or de ses traits.   8

Une Nymphe s'égare et s'arrête. Elle écoute
Les larmes du matin qui pleuvent goutte à goutte
Sur la mousse. L'ivresse emplit son jeune cœur.

Mais, d'un seul bond, le Dieu du noir taillis s'élance,   12
La saisit, frappe l'air de son rire moqueur,
Disparaît . . . Et les bois retombent au silence.

Le Bain des Nymphes

C'est un vallon sauvage abrité de l'Euxin;
Au-dessus de la source un noir laurier se penche,
Et la Nymphe, riant, suspendue à la branche,
Frôle d'un pied craintif l'eau froide du bassin.   4

Ses compagnes, d'un bond, à l'appel du buccin,
Dans l'onde jaillissante où s'ébat leur chair blanche,
Plongent, et de l'écume émergent une hanche,
De clairs cheveux, un torse ou la rose d'un sein.   8

Une gaîté divine emplit le grand bois sombre.
Mais deux yeux, brusquement, ont illuminé l'ombre.
Le Satyre! . . . Son rire épouvante leurs jeux;

Elles s'élancent. Tel, lorsqu'un corbeau sinistre   12
Croasse, sur le fleuve éperdument neigeux,
S'effarouche le vol des cygnes du Caÿstre.

Le Vase

L'ivoire est ciselé d'une main fine et telle
Que l'on voit les forêts de Colchide et Jason
Et Médée aux grands yeux magiques. La Toison
Repose, étincelante, au sommet d'une stèle.   4

Auprès d'eux est couché le Nil, source immortelle
Des fleuves, et, plus loin, ivres du doux poison,
Les Bacchantes, d'un pampre à l'ample frondaison
Enguirlandent le joug des taureaux qu'on dételle.   8

Au-dessous, c'est un choc hurlant de cavaliers;
Puis les héros rentrant morts sur leurs boucliers
Et les vieillards plaintifs et les larmes des mères.

Enfin, en forme d'anse arrondissant leurs flancs,   12
Et posant aux deux bords leurs seins fermes et blancs,
Dans le vase sans fond s'abreuvent des Chimères.

Ariane

Au choc clair et vibrant des cymbales d'airain,
Nue, allongée au dos d'un grand tigre, la Reine
Regarde, avec l'Orgie immense qu'il entraîne,
Iacchos s'avancer sur le sable marin.   4

Et le monstre royal, ployant son large rein,
Sous le poids adoré foule la blonde arène,
Et, frôlé par la main d'où pend l'errante rêne,
En rugissant d'amour mord les fleurs de son frein.   8

Laissant sa chevelure à son flanc qui se cambre
Parmi les noirs raisins rouler ses grappes d'ambre,
L'Epouse n'entend pas le sourd rugissement;

Et sa bouche éperdue, ivre enfin d'ambroisie,   12
Oubliant ses longs cris vers l'infidèle amant,
Rit au baiser prochain du Dompteur de l'Asie.

Bacchanale

Une brusque clameur épouvante le Gange.
Les tigres ont rompu leurs jougs et, miaulants,
Ils bondissent, et sous leurs bonds et leurs élans
Les Bacchantes en fuite écrasent la vendange. 4

Et le pampre que l'ongle ou la morsure effrange
Rougit d'un noir raisin les gorges et les flancs
Où près des reins rayés luisent des ventres blancs
De léopards roulés dans la pourpre et la fange. 8

Sur les corps convulsifs les fauves éblouis,
Avec des grondements que prolonge un long râle,
Flairent un sang plus rouge à travers l'or du hâle ;

Mais le Dieu, s'enivrant à ces jeux inouïs, 12
Par le thyrse et les cris les exaspère et mêle
Au mâle rugissant la hurlante femelle.

Le Réveil d'un Dieu

La chevelure éparse et la gorge meurtrie,
Irritant par les pleurs l'ivresse de leurs sens,
Les femmes de Byblos, en lugubres accents,
Mènent la funéraire et lente théorie. 4

Car sur le lit jonché d'anémone fleurie
Où la Mort avait clos ses longs yeux languissants,
Repose, parfumé d'aromate et d'encens,
Le jeune homme adoré des vierges de Syrie. 8

Jusqu'à l'aurore ainsi le chœur s'est lamenté.
Mais voici qu'il s'éveille à l'appel d'Astarté,
L'Epoux mystérieux que le cinname arrose.

Il est ressuscité, l'antique adolescent ! 12
Et le ciel tout en fleur semble une immense rose
Qu'un Adonis céleste a teinte de son sang.

La Magicienne

En tous lieux, même au pied des autels que j'embrasse,
Je la vois qui m'appelle et m'ouvre ses bras blancs.
O père vénérable, ô mère dont les flancs
M'ont porté, suis-je né d'une exécrable race ?　　　　　4

L'Eumolpide vengeur n'a point dans Samothrace
Secoué vers le seuil les longs manteaux sanglants,
Et, malgré moi, je fuis, le cœur las, les pieds lents;
J'entends les chiens sacrés qui hurlent sur ma trace.　　8

Partout je sens, j'aspire, à moi-même odieux,
Les noirs enchantements et les sinistres charmes
Dont m'enveloppe encor la colère des Dieux;

Car les grands Dieux ont fait d'irrésistibles armes　　12
De sa bouche enivrante et de ses sombres yeux,
Pour armer contre moi ses baisers et ses larmes.

Sphinx

Au flanc du Cythéron, sous la ronce enfoui,
Le roc s'ouvre, repaire où resplendit au centre
Par l'éclat des yeux d'or, de la gorge et du ventre,
La Vierge aux ailes d'aigle et dont nul n'a joui.　　　4

Et l'Homme s'arrêta sur le seuil, ébloui.
—Quelle est l'ombre qui rend plus sombre encor mon antre ?
—L'Amour.—Es-tu le Dieu ?—Je suis le Héros.—Entre;
Mais tu cherches la mort. L'oses-tu braver ?—Oui.　　8

Bellérophon dompta la Chimère farouche.
—N'approche pas.—Ma lèvre a fait frémir ta bouche . . .
—Viens donc! Entre mes bras tes os vont se briser;

Mes ongles dans ta chair . . .—Qu'importe le supplice,　12
Si j'ai conquis la gloire et ravi le baiser?
—Tu triomphes en vain, car tu meurs.—O délice! . . .

Marsyas

Les pins du bois natal que charmait ton haleine
N'ont pas brûlé ta chair, ô malheureux! Tes os
Sont dissous, et ton sang s'écoule avec les eaux
Que les monts de Phrygie épanchent vers la plaine.   4

Le jaloux Citharède, orgueil du ciel hellène,
De son plectre de fer a brisé tes roseaux
Qui, domptant les lions, enseignaient les oiseaux;
Il ne reste plus rien du chanteur de Célène.   8

Rien qu'un lambeau sanglant qui flotte au tronc de l'if
Auquel on l'a lié pour l'écorcher tout vif.
O Dieu cruel! O cris! Voix lamentable et tendre!

Non, vous n'entendrez plus, sous un doigt trop savant,   12
La flûte soupirer aux rives du Méandre . . .
Car la peau du Satyre est le jouet du vent.

PERSEE ET ANDROMEDE

Andromède au Monstre

La Vierge Céphéenne, hélas! encor vivante,
Liée, échevelée, au roc des noirs îlots,
Se lamente en tordant avec de vains sanglots
Sa chair royale où court un frisson d'épouvante.   4

L'Océan monstrueux que la tempête évente
Crache à ses pieds glacés l'âcre bave des flots,
Et partout elle voit, à travers ses cils clos,
Bâiller la gueule glauque, innombrable et mouvante.   8

Tel qu'un éclat de foudre en un ciel sans éclair,
Tout à coup, retentit un hennissement clair.
Ses yeux s'ouvrent. L'horreur les emplit, et l'extase;

Car elle a vu, d'un vol vertigineux et sûr,   12
Se cabrant sous le poids du fils de Zeus, Pégase
Allonger sur la mer sa grande ombre d'azur.

Persée et Andromède

Au milieu de l'écume arrêtant son essor,
Le Cavalier vainqueur du monstre et de Méduse,
Ruisselant d'une bave horrible où le sang fuse,
Emporte entre ses bras la vierge aux cheveux d'or.   4

Sur l'étalon divin, frère de Chrysaor,
Qui piaffe dans la mer et hennit et refuse,
Il a posé l'Amante éperdue et confuse
Qui lui rit et l'étreint et qui sanglote encor.   8

Il l'embrasse. La houle enveloppe leur groupe.
Elle, d'un faible effort, ramène sur la croupe
Ses beaux pieds qu'en fuyant baise un flot vagabond ;

Mais Pégase irrité par le fouet de la lame,   12
A l'appel du Héros s'enlevant d'un seul bond,
Bat le ciel ébloui de ses ailes de flamme.

Le Ravissement d'Andromède

D'un vol silencieux, le grand Cheval ailé
Soufflant de ses naseaux élargis l'air qui fume,
Les emporte avec un frémissement de plume
A travers la nuit bleue et l'éther étoilé.   4

Ils vont. L'Afrique plonge au gouffre flagellé,
Puis l'Asie . . . un désert . . . le Liban ceint de brume . . .
Et voici qu'apparaît, toute blanche d'écume,
La mer mystérieuse où vint sombrer Hellé.   8

Et le vent gonfle ainsi que deux immenses voiles
Les ailes qui, volant d'étoiles en étoiles,
Aux amants enlacés font un tiède berceau ;

Tandis que, l'œil au ciel où palpite leur ombre,   12
Ils voient, irradiant du Bélier au Verseau,
Leurs constellations poindre dans l'azur sombre.

EPIGRAMMES ET BUCOLIQUES

Le Chevrier

O berger, ne suis pas dans cet âpre ravin
Les bonds capricieux de ce bouc indocile;
Aux pentes du Ménale, où l'été nous exile,
La nuit monte trop vite et ton espoir est vain. 4

Restons ici, veux-tu? J'ai des figues, du vin.
Nous attendrons le jour en ce sauvage asile.
Mais parle bas. Les Dieux sont partout, ô Mnasyle!
Hécate nous regarde avec son œil divin. 8

Ce trou d'ombre, là-bas, est l'antre où se retire
Le Démon familier des hauts lieux, le Satyre;
Peut-être il sortira, si nous ne l'effrayons.

Entends-tu le pipeau qui chante sur ses lèvres? 12
C'est lui! Sa double corne accroche les rayons,
Et, vois, au clair de lune il fait danser mes chèvres!

Les Bergers

Viens. Le sentier s'enfonce aux gorges du Cyllène;
Voici l'antre et la source, et c'est là qu'il se plaît
A dormir sur un lit d'herbe et de serpolet
A l'ombre du grand pin où chante son haleine.   4

Attache à ce vieux tronc moussu la brebis pleine.
Sais-tu qu'avant un mois, avec son agnelet,
Elle lui donnera des fromages, du lait?
Les Nymphes fileront un manteau de sa laine.   8

Sois-nous propice, Pan! ô Chèvre-pied, gardien
Des troupeaux que nourrit le mont Arcadien,
Je t'invoque . . . Il entend! J'ai vu tressaillir l'arbre.

Partons. Le soleil plonge au couchant radieux.   12
Le don du pauvre, ami, vaut un autel de marbre,
Si d'un cœur simple et pur l'offrande est faite aux Dieux.

Epigramme votive

Au rude Arès! A la belliqueuse Discorde!
Aide-moi, je suis vieux, à suspendre au pilier
Mes glaives ébréchés et mon lourd bouclier,
Et ce casque rompu qu'un crin sanglant déborde.   4

Joins-y cet arc. Mais, dis, convient-il que je torde
Le chanvre autour du bois?—c'est un dur néflier
Que nul autre jamais n'a su faire plier—
Ou que d'un bras tremblant je tende encor la corde?   8

Prends aussi le carquois. Ton œil semble chercher
En leur gaine de cuir les armes de l'archer,
Les flèches que le vent des batailles disperse;

Il est vide. Tu crois que j'ai perdu mes traits?   12
Au champ de Marathon tu les retrouverais,
Car ils y sont restés dans la gorge du Perse.

Epigramme funéraire

Ici gît, Etranger, la verte sauterelle
Que durant deux saisons nourrit la jeune Hellé,
Et dont l'aile vibrant sous le pied dentelé
Bruissait dans le pin, le cytise ou l'airelle.   4

Elle s'est tue, hélas! la lyre naturelle,
La muse des guérets, des sillons et du blé;
De peur que son léger sommeil ne soit troublé,
Ah! passe vite, ami, ne pèse point sur elle.   8

C'est là. Blanche, au milieu d'une touffe de thym,
Sa pierre funéraire est fraîchement posée.
Que d'hommes n'ont pas eu ce suprême destin!

Des larmes d'un enfant sa tombe est arrosée,   12
Et l'Aurore pieuse y fait chaque matin
Une libation de gouttes de rosée.

Le Naufragé

Avec la brise en poupe et par un ciel serein,
Voyant le Phare fuir à travers la mâture,
Il est parti d'Egypte au lever de l'Arcture,
Fier de sa nef rapide aux flancs doublés d'airain.   4

Il ne reverra plus le môle Alexandrin.
Dans le sable où pas même un chevreau ne pâture
La tempête a creusé sa triste sépulture;
Le vent du large y tord quelque arbuste marin.   8

Au pli le plus profond de la mouvante dune,
En la nuit sans aurore et sans astre et sans lune,
Que le navigateur trouve enfin le repos!

O Terre, ô Mer, pitié pour son ombre anxieuse!   12
Et sur la rive hellène où sont venus ses os,
Soyez-lui, toi, légère, et toi, silencieuse.

La Prière du Mort

Arrête! Ecoute-moi, voyageur. Si tes pas
Te portent vers Cypsèle et les rives de l'Hèbre,
Cherche le vieil Hyllos et dis-lui qu'il célèbre
Un long deuil pour le fils qu'il ne reverra pas.　　　　4

Ma chair assassinée a servi de repas
Aux loups. Le reste gît en ce hallier funèbre.
Et l'Ombre errante aux bords que l'Erèbe enténèbre
S'indigne et pleure. Nul n'a vengé mon trépas.　　　　8

Pars donc. Et si jamais, à l'heure où le jour tombe,
Tu rencontres au pied d'un tertre ou d'une tombe
Une femme au front blanc que voile un noir lambeau;

Approche-toi, ne crains ni la nuit ni les charmes;　　　12
C'est ma mère, Etranger, qui sur un vain tombeau
Embrasse une urne vide et l'emplit de ses larmes.

L'Esclave

Tel, nu, sordide, affreux, nourri des plus vils mets,
Esclave—vois, mon corps en a gardé les signes—
Je suis né libre au fond du golfe aux belles lignes
Où l'Hybla plein de miel mire ses bleus sommets.　　　4

J'ai quitté l'île heureuse, hélas!... Ah! si jamais
Vers Syracuse et les abeilles et les vignes
Tu retournes, suivant le vol vernal des cygnes,
Cher hôte, informe-toi de celle que j'aimais.　　　　8

Reverrai-je ses yeux de sombre violette,
Si purs, sourire au ciel natal qui s'y reflète
Sous l'arc victorieux que tend un sourcil noir?

Sois pitoyable! Pars, va, cherche Cléariste　　　　12
Et dis-lui que je vis encor pour la revoir.
Tu la reconnaîtras, car elle est toujours triste.

Le Laboureur

Le semoir, la charrue, un joug, des socs luisants,
La herse, l'aiguillon et la faulx acérée
Qui fauchait en un jour les épis d'une airée,
Et la fourche qui tend la gerbe aux paysans ;   4

Ces outils familiers, aujourd'hui trop pesants,
Le vieux Parmis les voue à l'immortelle Rhée
Par qui le germe éclôt sous la terre sacrée.
Pour lui, sa tâche est faite ; il a quatre-vingts ans.   8

Près d'un siècle, au soleil, sans en être plus riche,
Il a poussé le coutre au travers de la friche ;
Ayant vécu sans joie, il vieillit sans remords.

Mais il est las d'avoir tant peiné sur la glèbe   12
Et songe que peut-être il faudra, chez les morts,
Labourer des champs d'ombre arrosés par l'Erèbe.

A Hermès Criophore

Pour que le compagnon des Naïades se plaise
A rendre la brebis agréable au bélier
Et qu'il veuille par lui sans fin multiplier
L'errant troupeau qui broute aux berges du Galèse ;   4

Il faut lui faire fête et qu'il se sente à l'aise
Sous le toit de roseaux du pâtre hospitalier ;
Le sacrifice est doux au Démon familier
Sur la table de marbre ou sur un bloc de glaise.   8

Donc, honorons Hermès. Le subtil Immortel
Préfère à la splendeur du temple et de l'autel
La main pure immolant la victime impollue.

Ami, dressons un tertre aux bornes de ton pré   12
Et qu'un vieux bouc, du sang de sa gorge velue,
Fasse l'argile noire et le gazon pourpré.

La jeune Morte

Qui que tu sois, Vivant, passe vite parmi
L'herbe du tertre où gît ma cendre inconsolée;
Ne foule point les fleurs de l'humble mausolée
D'où j'écoute ramper le lierre et la fourmi.   4

Tu t'arrêtes? Un chant de colombe a gémi.
Non! qu'elle ne soit pas sur ma tombe immolée!
Si tu veux m'être cher, donne-lui la volée.
La vie est si douce, ah! laisse-la vivre, ami.   8

Le sais-tu? sous le myrte enguirlandant la porte,
Epouse et vierge, au seuil nuptial, je suis morte,
Si proche et déjà loin de celui que j'aimais.

Mes yeux se sont fermés à la lumière heureuse,   12
Et maintenant j'habite, hélas! et pour jamais,
L'inexorable Erèbe et la Nuit Ténébreuse.

Regilla

Passant, ce marbre couvre Annia Regilla
Du sang de Ganymède et d'Aphrodite née.
Le noble Hérode aima cette fille d'Enée.
Heureuse, jeune et belle, elle est morte. Plains-la.   4

Car l'Ombre dont le corps délicieux gît là,
Chez le prince infernal de l'Ile Fortunée
Compte les jours, les mois et la si longue année
Depuis que loin des siens la Parque l'exila.   8

Hanté du souvenir de sa forme charmante,
L'Epoux désespéré se lamente et tourmente
La pourpre sans sommeil du lit d'ivoire et d'or.

Il tarde. Il ne vient pas. Et l'âme de l'Amante,   12
Anxieuse, espérant qu'il vienne, vole encor
Autour du sceptre noir que lève Rhadamanthe.

Le Coureur

Tel que Delphes l'a vu quand, Thymos le suivant,
Il volait par le stade aux clameurs de la foule,
Tel Ladas court encor sur le socle qu'il foule
D'un pied de bronze, svelte et plus vif que le vent.   4

Le bras tendu, l'œil fixe et le torse en avant,
Une sueur d'airain à son front perle et coule ;
On dirait que l'athlète a jailli hors du moule,
Tandis que le sculpteur le fondait, tout vivant.   8

Il palpite, il frémit d'espérance et de fièvre,
Son flanc halète, l'air qu'il fend manque à sa lèvre
Et l'effort fait saillir ses muscles de métal ;

L'irrésistible élan de la course l'entraîne   12
Et passant par-dessus son propre piédestal,
Vers la palme et le but il va fuir dans l'arène.

Le Cocher

Etranger, celui qui, debout au timon d'or,
Maîtrise d'une main par leur quadruple rêne
Ses chevaux noirs et tient de l'autre un fouet de frêne,
Guide un quadrige mieux que le héros Castor.   4

Issu d'un père illustre et plus illustre encor . . .
Mais vers la borne rouge où la course l'entraîne,
Il part, semant déjà ses rivaux sur l'arène,
Le Libyen hardi cher à l'Autocrator.   8

Dans le cirque ébloui, vers le but et la palme,
Sept fois, triomphateur vertigineux et calme,
Il a tourné. Salut, fils de Calchas le Bleu !

Et tu vas voir, si l'œil d'un mortel peut suffire   12
A cette apothéose où fuit un char de feu,
La Victoire voler pour rejoindre Porphyre.

Sur l'Othrys

L'air fraîchit. Le soleil plonge au ciel radieux.
Le bétail ne craint plus le taon ni le bupreste.
Aux pentes de l'Othrys l'ombre est plus longue. Reste,
Reste avec moi, cher hôte envoyé par les Dieux.   4

Tandis que tu boiras un lait fumant, tes yeux
Contempleront du seuil de ma cabane agreste,
Des cimes de l'Olympe aux neiges du Thymphreste,
La riche Thessalie et les monts glorieux.   8

Vois la mer et l'Eubée et, rouge au crépuscule,
Le Callidrome sombre et l'Œta, dont Hercule
Fit son bûcher suprême et son premier autel;

Et là-bas, à travers la lumineuse gaze,   12
Le Parnasse où, le soir, las d'un vol immortel,
Se pose, et d'où s'envole, à l'aurore, Pégase!

ROME ET LES BARBARES

Pour le Vaisseau de Virgile

Que vos astres plus clairs gardent mieux du danger,
Dioscures brillants, divins frères d'Hélène,
Le poète latin qui veut, au ciel hellène,
Voir les Cyclades d'or de l'azur émerger.   4

Que des souffles de l'air, de tous le plus léger,
Que le doux Iapyx, redoublant son haleine,
D'une brise embaumée enfle la voile pleine
Et pousse le navire au rivage étranger.   8

A travers l'Archipel où le dauphin se joue,
Guidez heureusement le chanteur de Mantoue;
Prêtez-lui, fils du Cygne, un fraternel rayon.

La moitié de mon âme est dans la nef fragile   12
Qui, sur la mer sacrée où chantait Arion,
Vers la terre des Dieux porte le grand Virgile.

Villula

Oui, c'est au vieux Gallus qu'appartient l'héritage
Que tu vois au penchant du coteau cisalpin;
La maison tout entière est à l'abri d'un pin
Et le chaume du toit couvre à peine un étage. 4

Il suffit pour qu'un hôte avec lui le partage.
Il a sa vigne, un four à cuire plus d'un pain,
Et dans son potager foisonne le lupin.
C'est peu? Gallus n'a pas désiré davantage. 8

Son bois donne un fagot ou deux tous les hivers,
Et de l'ombre, l'été, sous les feuillages verts;
A l'automne on y prend quelque grive au passage.

C'est là que, satisfait de son destin borné, 12
Gallus finit de vivre où jadis il est né.
Va, tu sais à présent que Gallus est un sage.

La Flûte

Voici le soir. Au ciel passe un vol de pigeons.
Rien ne vaut pour charmer une amoureuse fièvre,
O chevrier, le son d'un pipeau sur la lèvre
Qu'accompagne un bruit frais de source entre les joncs. 4

A l'ombre du platane où nous nous allongeons
L'herbe est plus molle. Laisse, ami, l'errante chèvre,
Sourde aux chevrotements du chevreau qu'elle sèvre,
Escalader la roche et brouter les bourgeons. 8

Ma flûte, faite avec sept tiges de ciguë
Inégales que joint un peu de cire, aiguë
Ou grave, pleure, chante ou gémit à mon gré.

Viens. Nous t'enseignerons l'art divin du Silène, 12
Et tes soupirs d'amour, de ce tuyau sacré,
S'envoleront parmi l'harmonieuse haleine.

A Sextius

Le ciel est clair. La barque a glissé sur les sables.
Les vergers sont fleuris et le givre argentin
N'irise plus les prés au soleil du matin.
Les bœufs et le bouvier désertent les étables.　　　　4

Tout renaît. Mais la Mort et ses funèbres fables
Nous pressent, et, pour toi, seul le jour est certain
Où les dés renversés en un libre festin
Ne t'assigneront plus la royauté des tables.　　　　8

La vie, ô Sextius, est brève. Hâtons-nous
De vivre. Déjà l'âge a rompu nos genoux.
Il n'est pas de printemps au froid pays des Ombres.

Viens donc. Les bois sont verts, et voici la saison　　　12
D'immoler à Faunus, en ses retraites sombres,
Un bouc noir ou l'agnelle à la blanche toison.

HORTORUM DEUS

I

Olim truncus eram ficulnus.
Horace.

A Paul Arène

N'approche pas! Va-t'en! Passe au large, Etranger!
Insidieux pillard, tu voudrais, j'imagine,
Dérober les raisins, l'olive ou l'aubergine
Que le soleil mûrit à l'ombre du verger?   4

J'y veille. A coups de serpe, autrefois, un berger
M'a taillé dans le tronc d'un dur figuier d'Egine;
Ris du sculpteur, Passant, mais songe à l'origine
De Priape, et qu'il peut rudement se venger.   8

Jadis, cher aux marins, sur un bec de galère
Je me dressais, vermeil, joyeux de la colère
Ecumante ou du rire éblouissant des flots;

A présent, vil gardien de fruits et de salades,   12
Contre les maraudeurs je défends cet enclos . . .
Et je ne verrai plus les riantes Cyclades.

II

Hujus nam domini colunt me Deumque salutant.
Catulle.

Respecte, ô Voyageur, si tu crains ma colère,
Cet humble toit de joncs tressés et de glaïeul.
Là, parmi ses enfants, vit un robuste aïeul;
C'est le maître du clos et de la source claire.　　4

Et c'est lui qui planta droit au milieu de l'aire
Mon emblème équarri dans un cœur de tilleul;
Il n'a point d'autres Dieux, aussi je garde seul
Le verger qu'il cultive et fleurit pour me plaire.　　8

Ce sont de pauvres gens, rustiques et dévots.
Par eux, la violette et les sombres pavots
Ornent ma gaine avec les verts épis de l'orge;

Et toujours, deux fois l'an, l'agreste autel a bu,　　12
Sous le couteau sacré du colon qui l'égorge,
Le sang d'un jeune bouc impudique et barbu.

III

*Ecce villicus
Venit . . .*
Catulle.

Holà, maudits enfants! Gare au piège, à la trappe,
Au chien! Je ne veux plus, moi qui garde ce lieu,
Qu'on vienne, sous couleur d'y querir un caïeu
D'ail, piller mes fruitiers et grappiller ma grappe.　　4

D'ailleurs, là-bas, du fond des chaumes qu'il étrape,
Le colon vous épie, et, s'il vient, par mon pieu!
Vos reins sauront alors tout ce que pèse un Dieu
De bois dur emmanché d'un bras d'homme qui frappe.　　8

Vite, prenez la sente à gauche, suivez-la
Jusqu'au bout de la haie où croît ce hêtre, et là
Profitez de l'avis qu'on vous glisse à l'oreille:

Un négligent Priape habite au clos voisin. 12
D'ici, vous pouvez voir les piliers de sa treille
Où sous l'ombre du pampre a rougi le raisin.

IV

Mihi corolla picta vere ponitur.
Catulle.

Entre donc. Mes piliers sont fraîchement crépis,
Et sous ma treille neuve où le soleil se glisse
L'ombre est plus douce. L'air embaume la mélisse.
Avril jonche la terre en fleur d'un frais tapis. 4

Les saisons tour à tour me parent: blonds épis,
Raisins mûrs, verte olive ou printanier calice;
Et le lait du matin caille encor sur l'éclisse
Que la chèvre me tend la mamelle et le pis. 8

Le maître de ce clos m'honore. J'en suis digne.
Jamais grive ou larron ne marauda sa vigne
Et nul n'est mieux gardé de tout le Champ Romain.

Les fils sont beaux, la femme est vertueuse, et l'homme, 12
Chaque soir de marché, fait tinter dans sa main
Les deniers d'argent clair qu'il rapporte de Rome.

V

Rigetque dura barba juncta crystallo.
Diversorum Poetarum Lusus.

Quel froid ! le givre brille aux derniers pampres verts ;
Je guette le soleil, car je sais l'heure exacte
Où l'aurore rougit les neiges du Soracte.
Le sort d'un Dieu champêtre est dur. L'homme est pervers.　　4

Dans ce clos ruiné, seul, depuis vingt hivers
Je me morfonds. Ma barbe est hirsute et compacte,
Mon vermillon s'écaille et mon bois se rétracte
Et se gerce, et j'ai peur d'être piqué des vers.　　8

Que ne suis-je un Pénate ou même simple Lare
Domestique, repeint, repu, toujours hilare,
Gorgé de miel, de fruits ou ceint des fleurs d'avril !

Près des aïeux de cire, au fond du vestibule,　　12
Je vieillirais et les enfants, au jour viril,
A mon col vénéré viendraient pendre leur bulle.

Le Tepidarium

La myrrhe a parfumé leurs membres assouplis ;
Elles rêvent, goûtant la tiédeur de Décembre,
Et le brasier de bronze illuminant la chambre
Jette la flamme et l'ombre à leurs beaux fronts pâlis.   4

Aux coussins de byssus, dans la pourpre des lits,
Sans bruit, parfois un corps de marbre rose ou d'ambre
Ou se soulève à peine ou s'allonge ou se cambre ;
Le lin voluptueux dessine de longs plis.   8

Sentant à sa chair nue errer l'ardent effluve,
Une femme d'Asie, au milieu de l'étuve,
Tord ses bras énervés en un ennui serein ;

Et le pâle troupeau des filles d'Ausonie   12
S'enivre de la riche et sauvage harmonie
Des noirs cheveux roulant sur un torse d'airain.

Tranquillus

C. Plinii Secundi Epist. Lib. I, Ep. xxiv.

C'est dans ce doux pays qu'a vécu Suétone;
Et de l'humble villa voisine de Tibur,
Parmi la vigne, il reste encore un pan de mur,
Un arceau ruiné que le pampre festonne.   4

C'est là qu'il se plaisait à venir, chaque automne,
Loin de Rome, aux rayons des derniers ciels d'azur,
Vendanger ses ormeaux qu'alourdit le cep mûr.
Là sa vie a coulé tranquille et monotone.   8

Au milieu de la paix pastorale, c'est là
Que l'ont hanté Néron, Claude, Caligula,
Messaline rôdant sous la stole pourprée;

Et que, du fer d'un style à la pointe acérée   12
Egratignant la cire impitoyable, il a
Décrit les noirs loisirs du vieillard de Caprée.

Lupercus

M. Val. Martialis Lib. I, Epigr. cxviii.

Lupercus, du plus loin qu'il me voit:—Cher poète,
Ta nouvelle épigramme est du meilleur latin;
Dis, veux-tu, j'enverrai chez toi demain matin,
Me prêter les rouleaux de ton œuvre complète?   4

—Non. Ton esclave boite, il est vieux, il halète,
Mes escaliers sont durs et mon logis lointain;
Ne demeures-tu pas auprès du Palatin?
Atrectus, mon libraire, habite l'Argilète.   8

Sa boutique est au coin du Forum. Il y vend
Les volumes des morts et celui du vivant,
Virgile et Silius, Pline, Térence ou Phèdre;

Là, sur l'un des rayons, et non certe aux derniers,   12
Poncé, vêtu de pourpre et dans un nid de cèdre,
Martial est en vente au prix de cinq deniers.

La Trebbia

L'aube d'un jour sinistre a blanchi les hauteurs.
Le camp s'éveille. En bas roule et gronde le fleuve
Où l'escadron léger des Numides s'abreuve.
Partout sonne l'appel clair des buccinateurs.   4

Car malgré Scipion, les augures menteurs,
La Trebbia débordée, et qu'il vente et qu'il pleuve,
Sempronius Consul, fier de sa gloire neuve,
A fait lever la hache et marcher les licteurs.   8

Rougissant le ciel noir de flamboîments lugubres,
A l'horizon, brûlaient les villages Insubres;
On entendait au loin barrir un éléphant.

Et là-bas, sous le pont, adossé contre une arche,   12
Hannibal écoutait, pensif et triomphant,
Le piétinement sourd des légions en marche.

Après Cannes

Un des consuls tué, l'autre fuit vers Linterne
Ou Venuse. L'Aufide a débordé, trop plein
De morts et d'armes. La foudre au Capitolin
Tombe, le bronze sue et le ciel rouge est terne.   4

En vain le Grand Pontife a fait un lectisterne
Et consulté deux fois l'oracle sibyllin;
D'un long sanglot l'aïeul, la veuve, l'orphelin
Emplissent Rome en deuil que la terreur consterne.   8

Et chaque soir la foule allait aux aqueducs,
Plèbe, esclaves, enfants, femmes, vieillards caducs
Et tout ce que vomit Subure et l'ergastule;

Tous anxieux de voir surgir, au dos vermeil   12
Des monts Sabins où luit l'œil sanglant du soleil,
Le Chef borgne monté sur l'éléphant Gétule.

A un Triomphateur

Fais sculpter sur ton arc, Imperator illustre,
Des files de guerriers barbares, de vieux chefs
Sous le joug, des tronçons d'armures et de nefs,
Et la flotte captive et le rostre et l'aplustre.   4

Quel que tu sois, issu d'Ancus ou né d'un rustre,
Tes noms, famille, honneurs et titres, longs ou brefs,
Grave-les dans la frise et dans les bas-reliefs
Profondément, de peur que l'avenir te frustre.   8

Déjà le Temps brandit l'arme fatale. As-tu
L'espoir d'éterniser le bruit de ta vertu ?
Un vil lierre suffit à disjoindre un trophée ;

Et seul, aux blocs épars des marbres triomphaux   12
Où ta gloire en ruine est par l'herbe étouffée,
Quelque faucheur Samnite ébréchera sa faulx.

ANTOINE ET CLEOPATRE

Le Cydnus

Sous l'azur triomphal, au soleil qui flamboie,
La trirème d'argent blanchit le fleuve noir
Et son sillage y laisse un parfum d'encensoir
Avec des sons de flûte et des frissons de soie.   4

A la proue éclatante où l'épervier s'éploie,
Hors de son dais royal se penchant pour mieux voir,
Cléopâtre debout en la splendeur du soir
Semble un grand oiseau d'or qui guette au loin sa proie.   8

Voici Tarse, où l'attend le guerrier désarmé;
Et la brune Lagide ouvre dans l'air charmé
Ses bras d'ambre où la pourpre a mis des reflets roses.

Et ses yeux n'ont pas vu, présages de son sort,   12
Auprès d'elle, effeuillant sur l'eau sombre des roses,
Les deux enfants divins, le Désir et la Mort.

Soir de Bataille

Le choc avait été très rude. Les tribuns
Et les centurions, ralliant les cohortes,
Humaient encor dans l'air où vibraient leurs voix fortes
La chaleur du carnage et ses âcres parfums.   4

D'un œil morne, comptant leurs compagnons défunts,
Les soldats regardaient, comme des feuilles mortes,
Au loin, tourbillonner les archers de Phraortes;
Et la sueur coulait de leurs visages bruns.   8

C'est alors qu'apparut, tout hérissé de flèches,
Rouge du flux vermeil de ses blessures fraîches,
Sous la pourpre flottante et l'airain rutilant,

Au fracas des buccins qui sonnaient leur fanfare,   12
Superbe, maîtrisant son cheval qui s'effare,
Sur le ciel enflammé, l'Imperator sanglant.

Antoine et Cléopâtre

Tous deux ils regardaient, de la haute terrasse,
L'Egypte s'endormir sous un ciel étouffant
Et le Fleuve, à travers le Delta noir qu'il fend,
Vers Bubaste ou Saïs rouler son onde grasse.   4

Et le Romain sentait sous la lourde cuirasse,
Soldat captif berçant le sommeil d'un enfant,
Ployer et défaillir sur son cœur triomphant
Le corps voluptueux que son étreinte embrasse.   8

Tournant sa tête pâle entre ses cheveux bruns
Vers celui qu'enivraient d'invincibles parfums,
Elle tendit sa bouche et ses prunelles claires;

Et sur elle courbé, l'ardent Imperator   12
Vit dans ses larges yeux étoilés de points d'or
Toute une mer immense où fuyaient des galères.

SONNETS EPIGRAPHIQUES

Le Vœu

ILIXONI	ISCITTO DEO
DEO	HVNNV
FAB. FESTA	VLOHOXIS
V.S.L.M.	FIL.
	V.S.L.M.

Jadis l'Ibère noir et le Gall au poil fauve
Et le Garumne brun peint d'ocre et de carmin,
Sur le marbre votif entaillé par leur main,
Ont dit l'eau bienfaisante et sa vertu qui sauve.   4

Puis les Imperators, sous le Venasque chauve,
Bâtirent la piscine et le therme romain,
Et Fabia Festa, par ce même chemin,
A cueilli pour les Dieux la verveine ou la mauve.   8

Aujourd'hui, comme aux jours d'Iscitt et d'Ilixon,
Les sources m'ont chanté leur divine chanson;
Le soufre fume encore à l'air pur des moraines.

C'est pourquoi, dans ces vers, accomplissant les vœux,   12
Tel qu'autrefois Hunnu, fils d'Ulohox, je veux
Dresser l'autel barbare aux Nymphes Souterraines.

La Source

NYMPHIS. AVG. SACRVM.

L'autel gît sous la ronce et l'herbe enseveli;
Et la Source sans nom qui goutte à goutte tombe
D'un son plaintif emplit la solitaire combe.
C'est la Nymphe qui pleure un éternel oubli.   4

L'inutile miroir que ne ride aucun pli
A peine est effleuré par un vol de colombe
Et la lune, parfois, qui du ciel noir surplombe,
Seule, y reflète encore un visage pâli.   8

De loin en loin, un pâtre errant s'y désaltère.
Il boit, et sur la dalle antique du chemin
Verse un peu d'eau resté dans le creux de sa main.

Il a fait, malgré lui, le geste héréditaire,   12
Et ses yeux n'ont pas vu sur le cippe romain
Le vase libatoire auprès de la patère.

Le Dieu Hêtre

FAGO DEO.

Le Garumne a bâti sa rustique maison
Sous un grand hêtre au tronc musculeux comme un torse
Dont le sève d'un Dieu gonfle la blanche écorce.
La forêt maternelle est tout son horizon.   4

Car l'homme libre y trouve, au gré de la saison,
Les faînes, le bois, l'ombre, et les bêtes qu'il force
Avec l'arc ou l'épieu, le filet ou l'amorce,
Pour en manger la chair et vêtir leur toison.   8

Longtemps il a vécu riche, heureux et sans maître,
Et le soir, lorsqu'il rentre au logis, le vieux Hêtre
De ses bras familiers semble lui faire accueil;

Et quand la Mort viendra courber sa tête franche,   12
Ses petits-fils auront pour tailler son cercueil
L'incorruptible cœur de la maîtresse branche.

Aux Montagnes Divines

GEMINVS SERVVS
ET PRO SVIS CONSERVIS.

Glaciers bleus, pics de marbre et d'ardoise, granits,
Moraines dont le vent, du Néthou jusqu'à Bègle,
Arrache, brûle et tord le froment et le seigle,
Cols abrupts, lacs, forêts pleines d'ombre et de nids! 4

Antres sourds, noirs vallons que les anciens bannis,
Plutôt que de ployer sous la servile règle,
Hantèrent avec l'ours, le loup, l'isard et l'aigle,
Précipices, torrents, gouffres, soyez bénis! 8

Ayant fui l'ergastule et le dur municipe,
L'esclave Geminus a dédié ce cippe
Aux Monts, gardiens sacrés de l'âpre liberté;

Et sur ces sommets clairs où le silence vibre, 12
Dans l'air inviolable, immense et pur, jeté,
Je crois entendre encor le cri d'un homme libre!

L'Exilée

MONTIBVS...
GARRI DEO...
SABINVLA.
V.S.L.M.

Dans ce vallon sauvage où César t'exila,
Sur la roche moussue, au chemin d'Ardiège,
Penchant ton front qu'argente une précoce neige,
Chaque soir, à pas lents, tu viens t'accouder là.   4

Tu revois ta jeunesse et ta chère villa
Et le Flamine rouge avec son blanc cortège;
Et lorsque le regret du sol latin t'assiège,
Tu regardes le ciel, triste Sabinula.   8

Vers le Gar éclatant aux sept pointes calcaires,
Les aigles attardés qui regagnent leurs aires
Emportent en leur vol tes rêves familiers;

Et seule, sans désirs, n'espérant rien de l'homme,   12
Tu dresses des autels aux Monts hospitaliers
Dont les Dieux plus prochains te consolent de Rome.

LE MOYEN AGE ET LA RENAISSANCE

Vitrail

Cette verrière a vu dames et hauts barons
Etincelants d'azur, d'or, de flamme et de nacre
Incliner, sous la dextre auguste qui consacre,
L'orgueil de leurs cimiers et de leurs chaperons;   4

Lorsqu'ils allaient, au bruit du cor ou des clairons,
Ayant le glaive au poing, le gerfaut ou le sacre,
Vers la plaine ou le bois, Byzance ou Saint-Jean d'Acre,
Partir pour la croisade ou le vol des hérons.   8

Aujourd'hui, les seigneurs auprès des châtelaines,
Avec le lévrier à leurs longues poulaines,
S'allongent aux carreaux de marbre blanc et noir;

Ils gisent là sans voix, sans geste et sans ouïe,   12
Et de leurs yeux de pierre ils regardent sans voir
La rose du vitrail toujours épanouie.

Epiphanie

Donc, Balthazar, Melchior et Gaspar, les Rois Mages,
Chargés de nefs d'argent, de vermeil et d'émaux
Et suivis d'un très long cortège de chameaux,
S'avancent, tels qu'ils sont dans les vieilles images.   4

De l'Orient lointain, ils portent leurs hommages
Aux pieds du fils de Dieu né pour guérir les maux
Que souffrent ici-bas l'homme et les animaux;
Un page noir soutient leurs robes à ramages.   8

Sur le seuil de l'étable où veille saint Joseph,
Ils ôtent humblement la couronne du chef
Pour saluer l'Enfant qui rit et les admire.

C'est ainsi qu'autrefois, sous Augustus Cæsar,   12
Sont venus, présentant l'or, l'encens et la myrrhe,
Les Rois Mages Gaspar, Melchior et Balthazar.

Le Huchier de Nazareth

Le bon maître huchier, pour finir un dressoir,
Courbé sur l'établi depuis l'aurore ahane,
Maniant tour à tour le rabot, le bédane
Et la râpe grinçante ou le dur polissoir.   4

Aussi, non sans plaisir, a-t-il vu, vers le soir,
S'allonger jusqu'au seuil l'ombre du grand platane
Où madame la Vierge et sa mère sainte Anne
Et Monseigneur Jésus près de lui vont s'asseoir.   8

L'air est brûlant et pas une feuille ne bouge;
Et saint Joseph, très las, a laissé choir la gouge
En s'essuyant le front au coin du tablier;

Mais l'Apprenti divin qu'une gloire enveloppe   12
Fait toujours, dans le fond obscur de l'atelier,
Voler des copeaux d'or au fil de sa varlope.

L'Estoc

Au pommeau de l'épée on lit : Calixte Pape.
La tiare, les clefs, la barque et le tramail
Blasonnent, en reliefs d'un somptueux travail,
Le Bœuf héréditaire armoyé sur la chappe.   4

A la fusée, un dieu païen, Faune ou Priape,
Rit, engainé d'un lierre à graines de corail ;
Et l'éclat du métal s'exalte sous l'émail
Si clair, que l'estoc brille encor plus qu'il ne frappe.   8

Maître Antonio Perez de Las Cellas forgea
Ce bâton pastoral pour le premier Borja,
Comme s'il pressentait sa fameuse lignée ;

Et ce glaive dit mieux qu'Arioste ou Sannazar,   12
Par l'acier de sa lame et l'or de sa poignée,
Le pontife Alexandre et le prince César.

Médaille

Seigneur de Rimini, Vicaire et Podestà.
Son profil d'épervier vit, s'accuse ou recule
A la lueur d'airain d'un fauve crépuscule,
Dans l'orbe où Matteo de' Pastis l'incrusta.   4

Or, de tous les tyrans qu'un peuple détesta,
Nul, comte, marquis, duc, prince ou principicule,
Qu'il ait nom Ezzelin, Can, Galéas, Hercule,
Ne fut maître si fier que le Malatesta.   8

Celui-ci, le meilleur, ce Sigismond Pandolphe,
Mit à sang la Romagne et la Marche et le Golfe,
Bâtit un temple, fit l'amour et le chanta ;

Et leurs femmes aussi sont rudes et sévères,   12
Car sur le même bronze où sourit Isotta,
L'éléphant triomphal foule des primevères.

Suivant Pétrarque

Vous sortiez de l'église et, d'un geste pieux,
Vos nobles mains faisaient l'aumône au populaire
Et sous le porche obscur votre beauté si claire
Aux pauvres éblouis montrait tout l'or des cieux.   4

Et je vous saluai d'un salut gracieux,
Très humble, comme il sied à qui ne veut déplaire,
Quand, tirant votre mante et d'un air de colère
Vous détournant de moi, vous couvrîtes vos yeux.   8

Mais Amour qui commande au cœur le plus rebelle
Ne voulut pas souffrir que, moins tendre que belle,
La source de pitié me refusât merci;

Et vous fûtes si lente à ramener le voile,   12
Que vos cils ombrageux palpitèrent ainsi
Qu'un noir feuillage où filtre un long rayon d'étoile.

Sur le Livre des Amours de Pierre de Ronsard

Jadis plus d'un amant, aux jardins de Bourgueil,
A gravé plus d'un nom dans l'écorce qu'il ouvre,
Et plus d'un cœur, sous l'or des hauts plafonds du Louvre,
A l'éclair d'un sourire a tressailli d'orgueil.   4

Qu'importe? Rien n'a dit leur ivresse ou leur deuil,
Ils gisent tout entiers entre quatre ais de rouvre
Et nul n'a disputé, sous l'herbe qui les couvre,
Leur inerte poussière à l'oubli du cercueil.   8

Tout meurt. Marie, Hélène et toi, fière Cassandre,
Vos beaux corps ne seraient qu'une insensible cendre,
—Les roses et les lys n'ont pas de lendemain—

Si Ronsard, sur la Seine ou sur la blonde Loire,   12
N'eût tressé pour vos fronts, d'une immortelle main,
Aux myrtes de l'Amour le laurier de la Gloire.

La belle Viole

A vous trouppe légère
Qui d'aile passagère
Par le monde volez . . .
Joachim du Bellay.

Accoudée au balcon d'où l'on voit le chemin
Qui va des bords de Loire aux rives d'Italie,
Sous un pâle rameau d'olive son front plie.
La violette en fleur se fanera demain.   4

La viole que frôle encor sa frêle main
Charme sa solitude et sa mélancolie,
Et son rêve s'envole à celui qui l'oublie
En foulant la poussière où gît l'orgueil Romain.   8

De celle qu'il nommait sa douceur Angevine,
Sur la corde vibrante erre l'âme divine
Quand l'angoisse d'amour étreint son cœur troublé;

Et sa voix livre aux vents qui l'emportent loin d'elle,   12
Et le caresseront peut-être, l'infidèle,
Cette chanson qu'il fit pour un vanneur de blé.

Epitaphe

Suivant les vers de Henri III.

O passant, c'est ici que repose Hyacinthe
Qui fut de son vivant seigneur de Maugiron;
Il est mort—Dieu l'absolve et l'ait en son giron!
Tombé sur le terrain, il gît en terre sainte.   4

Nul, ni même Quélus, n'a mieux, de perles ceinte,
Porté la toque à plume ou la fraise à godron;
Aussi vois-tu, sculpté par un nouveau Myron,
Dans ce marbre funèbre un rameau de jacinthe.   8

Après l'avoir baisé, fait tondre, et de sa main
Mis au linceul, Henry voulut qu'à Saint-Germain
Fût porté ce beau corps, hélas! inerte et blême;

Et jaloux qu'un tel deuil dure éternellement,   12
Il lui fit en l'église ériger cet emblème,
Des regrets d'Apollo triste et doux monument.

Vélin doré

Vieux maître relieur, l'or que tu ciselas
Au dos du livre et dans l'épaisseur de la tranche
N'a plus, malgré les fers poussés d'une main franche,
La rutilante ardeur de ses premiers éclats.   4

Les chiffres enlacés que liait l'entrelacs
S'effacent chaque jour de la peau fine et blanche;
A peine si mes yeux peuvent suivre la branche
De lierre que tu fis serpenter sur les plats.   8

Mais cet ivoire souple et presque diaphane,
Marguerite, Marie, ou peut-être Diane,
De leurs doigts amoureux l'ont jadis caressé;

Et ce vélin pâli que dora Clovis Eve   12
Evoque, je ne sais par quel charme passé,
L'âme de leur parfum et l'ombre de leur rêve.

La Dogaresse

Le palais est de marbre où, le long des portiques,
Conversent des seigneurs que peignit Titien,
Et les colliers massifs au poids du marc ancien
Rehaussent la splendeur des rouges dalmatiques.   4

Ils regardent au fond des lagunes antiques,
De leurs yeux où reluit l'orgueil patricien,
Sous le pavillon clair du ciel vénitien
Etinceler l'azur des mers Adriatiques.   8

Et tandis que l'essaim brillant des cavaliers
Traîne la pourpre et l'or par les blancs escaliers
Joyeusement baignés d'une lumière bleue;

Indolente et superbe, une Dame, à l'écart,   12
Se tournant à demi dans un flot de brocart,
Sourit au négrillon qui lui porte la queue.

Sur le Pont-Vieux

Antonio di Sandro orefice.

Le vaillant Maître Orfèvre, à l'œuvre dès matines,
Faisait, de ses pinceaux d'où s'égouttait l'émail,
Sur la paix niellée ou sur l'or du fermail
Epanouir la fleur des devises latines.   4

Sur le Pont, au son clair des cloches argentines,
La cape coudoyait le froc et le camail;
Et le soleil montant en un ciel de vitrail
Mettait un nimbe au front des belles Florentines.   8

Et prompts au rêve ardent qui les savait charmer,
Les apprentis, pensifs, oubliaient de fermer
Les mains des fiancés au chaton de la bague;

Tandis que d'un burin trempé comme un stylet,   12
Le jeune Cellini, sans rien voir, ciselait
Le combat des Titans au pommeau d'une dague.

Le vieil Orfèvre

Mieux qu'aucun maître inscrit au livre de maîtrise,
Qu'il ait nom Ruyz, Arphé, Ximeniz, Becerril,
J'ai serti le rubis, la perle et le béryl,
Tordu l'anse d'un vase et martelé sa frise.   4

Dans l'argent, sur l'émail où le paillon s'irise,
J'ai peint et j'ai sculpté, mettant l'âme en péril,
Au lieu de Christ en croix et du Saint sur le gril,
O honte! Bacchus ivre ou Danaé surprise.   8

J'ai de plus d'un estoc damasquiné le fer
Et, pour le vain orgueil de ces œuvres d'Enfer,
Aventuré ma part de l'éternelle Vie.

Aussi, voyant mon âge incliner vers le soir,   12
Je veux, ainsi que fit Fray Juan de Ségovie,
Mourir en ciselant dans l'or un ostensoir.

L'Epée

Crois-moi, pieux enfant, suis l'antique chemin.
L'épée aux quillons droits d'où part la branche torse,
Au poing d'un gentilhomme ardent et plein de force
Est un faix plus léger qu'un rituel romain.   4

Prends-la. L'Hercule d'or qui tiédit dans ta main,
Aux doigts de tes aïeux ayant poli son torse,
Gonfle plus fièrement, sous la splendide écorce,
Les beaux muscles de fer de son corps surhumain.   8

Brandis-la! L'acier souple en bouquets d'étincelles
Pétille. Elle est solide, et sa lame est de celles
Qui font courir au cœur un orgueilleux frisson;

Car elle porte au creux de sa brillante gorge,   12
Comme une noble Dame un joyau, le poinçon
De Julian del Rey, le prince de la forge.

A Claudius Popelin

Dans le cadre de plomb des fragiles verrières,
Les maîtres d'autrefois ont peint de hauts barons
Et, de leurs doigts pieux tournant leurs chaperons,
Ployé l'humble genou des bourgeois en prières.   4

D'autres sur le vélin jauni des bréviaires
Enluminaient des Saints parmi de beaux fleurons,
Ou laissaient rutiler, en traits souples et prompts,
Les arabesques d'or au ventre des aiguières.   8

Aujourd'hui Claudius, leur fils et leur rival,
Faisant revivre en lui ces ouvriers sublimes,
A fixé son génie au solide métal;

C'est pourquoi j'ai voulu, sous l'émail de mes rimes,   12
Faire autour de son front glorieux verdoyer,
Pou⌂ les âges futurs, l'héroïque laurier.

Email

Le four rougit; la plaque est prête. Prends ta lampe.
Modèle le paillon qui s'irise ardemment,
Et fixe avec le feu dans le sombre pigment
La poudre étincelante où ton pinceau se trempe.   4

Dis! ceindras-tu de myrte ou de laurier la tempe
Du penseur, du héros, du prince ou de l'amant?
Par quel Dieu feras-tu, sur un noir firmament,
Cabrer l'hydre écaillée ou le glauque hippocampe?   8

Non. Plutôt, en un orbe éclatant de saphir
Inscris un fier profil de guerrière d'Ophir,
Thalestris, Bradamante, Aude ou Penthésilée.

Et pour que sa beauté soit plus terrible encor,   12
Casque ses blonds cheveux de quelque bête ailée
Et fais bomber son sein sous la gorgone d'or.

Rêves d'Email

Ce soir, au réduit sombre où ronfle l'athanor,
Le grand feu prisonnier de la brique rougie
Exalte son ardeur et souffle sa magie
Au cuivre que l'émail fait plus riche que l'or.   4

Et sous mes pinceaux naît, vit, court et prend l'essor
Le peuple monstrueux de la mythologie,
Les Centaures, Pan, Sphinx, la Chimère, l'Orgie
Et, du sang de Gorgo, Pégase et Chrysaor.   8

Peindrai-je Achille en pleurs près de Penthésilée?
Orphée ouvrant les bras vers l'Epouse exilée
Sur la porte infernale aux infrangibles gonds?

Hercule terrassant le dogue de l'Averne,   12
Ou la Vierge qui tord au seuil de la caverne
Son corps épouvanté que flairent les Dragons?

LES CONQUERANTS

Les Conquérants

Comme un vol de gerfauts hors du charnier natal,
Fatigués de porter leurs misères hautaines,
De Palos de Moguer, routiers et capitaines
Partaient, ivres d'un rêve héroïque et brutal.   4

Ils allaient conquérir le fabuleux métal
Que Cipango mûrit dans ses mines lointaines,
Et les vents alizés inclinaient leurs antennes
Aux bords mystérieux du monde Occidental.   8

Chaque soir, espérant des lendemains épiques,
L'azur phosphorescent de la mer des Tropiques
Enchantait leur sommeil d'un mirage doré;

Ou penchés à l'avant des blanches caravelles,   12
Ils regardaient monter en un ciel ignoré
Du fond de l'Océan des étoiles nouvelles.

Jouvence

Juan Ponce de Leon, par le Diable tenté,
Déjà très vieux et plein des antiques études,
Voyant l'âge blanchir ses cheveux courts et rudes,
Prit la mer pour chercher la Source de Santé.   4

Sur sa belle Armada, d'un vain songe hanté,
Trois ans il explora les glauques solitudes,
Lorsque enfin, déchirant le brouillard des Bermudes,
La Floride apparut sous un ciel enchanté.   8

Et le Conquistador, bénissant sa folie,
Vint planter son pennon d'une main affaiblie
Dans la terre éclatante où s'ouvrait son tombeau.

Vieillard, tu fus heureux et ta fortune est telle   12
Que la Mort, malgré toi, fit ton rêve plus beau;
La Gloire t'a donné la Jeunesse immortelle.

Le Tombeau du Conquérant

A l'ombre de la voûte en fleur des catalpas
Et des tulipiers noirs qu'étoile un blanc pétale,
Il ne repose point dans la terre fatale;
La Floride conquise a manqué sous ses pas.   4

Un vil tombeau messied à de pareils trépas.
Linceul du Conquérant de l'Inde Occidentale,
Tout le Meschacébé par-dessus lui s'étale.
Le Peau Rouge et l'ours gris ne le troubleront pas.   8

Il dort au lit profond creusé par les eaux vierges.
Qu'importe un monument funéraire, des cierges,
Le psaume et la chapelle ardente et l'ex-voto?

Puisque le vent du Nord, parmi les cyprières,   12
Pleure et chante à jamais d'éternelles prières
Sur le Grand Fleuve où gît Hernando de Soto.

Carolo Quinto imperante

Celui-là peut compter parmi les grands défunts,
Car son bras a guidé la première carène
A travers l'archipel des Jardins de la Reine
Où la brise éternelle est faite de parfums.   4

Plus que les ans, la houle et ses âcres embruns,
Les calmes de la mer embrasée et sereine
Et l'amour et l'effroi de l'antique sirène
Ont fait sa barbe blanche et blancs ses cheveux bruns. 8

Castille a triomphé par cet homme, et ses flottes
Ont sous lui complété l'empire sans pareil
Pour lequel ne pouvait se coucher le soleil;

C'est Bartolomé Ruiz, prince des vieux pilotes,   12
Qui, sur l'écu royal qu'elle enrichit encor,
Porte une ancre de sable à la gumène d'or.

L'Ancêtre

A Claudius Popelin.

La gloire a sillonné de ses illustres rides
Le visage hardi de ce grand Cavalier
Qui porte sur son front que nul n'a fait plier
Le hâle de la guerre et des soleils torrides.   4

En tous lieux, Côte-Ferme, îles, sierras arides,
Il a planté la croix, et, depuis l'escalier
Des Andes, promené son pennon familier
Jusqu'au golfe orageux qui blanchit les Florides.   8

Pour ses derniers neveux, Claudius, tes pinceaux,
Sous l'armure de bronze aux splendides rinceaux,
Font revivre l'aïeul fier et mélancolique;

Et ses yeux assombris semblent chercher encor   12
Dans le ciel de l'émail ardent et métallique
Les éblouissements de la Castille d'Or.

A un Fondateur de ville

Las de poursuivre en vain l'Ophir insaisissable,
Tu fondas, en un pli de ce golfe enchanté
Où l'étendard royal par tes mains fut planté,
Une Carthage neuve au pays de la Fable.   4

Tu voulais que ton nom ne fût point périssable,
Et tu crus l'avoir bien pour toujours cimenté
A ce mortier sanglant dont tu fis ta cité;
Mais ton espoir, soldat, fut bâti sur le sable.   8

Carthagène étouffant sous le torride azur,
Avec ses noirs palais voit s'écrouler ton mur
Dans l'Océan fiévreux qui dévore sa grève;

Et seule, à ton cimier brille, ô Conquistador,   12
Héraldique témoin des splendeurs de ton rêve,
Une Ville d'argent qu'ombrage un palmier d'or.

Au Même

Qu'ils aient vaincu l'Inca, l'Aztèque, les Hiaquis,
Les Andes, la forêt, les pampas ou le fleuve,
Les autres n'ont laissé pour vestige et pour preuve
Qu'un nom, un titre vain de comte ou de marquis.   4

Toi, tu fondas, orgueil du sang dont je naquis,
Dans la mer caraïbe une Carthage neuve,
Et du Magdalena jusqu'au Darien qu'abreuve
L'Atrato, le sol rouge à la croix fut conquis.   8

Assise sur son île où l'Océan déferle,
Malgré les siècles, l'homme et la foudre et les vents,
Ta cité dresse au ciel ses forts et ses couvents;

Aussi tes derniers fils, sans trèfle, ache ni perle,   12
Timbrent-ils leur écu d'un palmier ombrageant
De son panache d'or une Ville d'argent.

A une Ville morte

Cartagena de Indias.
1532—1583—1697.

Morne Ville, jadis reine des Océans!
Aujourd'hui le requin poursuit en paix les scombres
Et le nuage errant allonge seul des ombres
Sur ta rade où roulaient les galions géants.   4

Depuis Drake et l'assaut des Anglais mécréants,
Tes murs désemparés croulent en noirs décombres
Et, comme un glorieux collier de perles sombres,
Des boulets de Pointis montrent les trous béants.   8

Entre le ciel qui brûle et la mer qui moutonne,
Au somnolent soleil d'un midi monotone,
Tu songes, ô Guerrière, aux vieux Conquistadors;

Et, dans l'énervement des nuits chaudes et calmes,   12
Berçant ta gloire éteinte, ô Cité, tu t'endors
Sous les palmiers, au long frémissement des palmes.

L'ORIENT ET LES TROPIQUES

LA VISION DE KHEM

I

Midi. L'air brûle et sous la terrible lumière
Le vieux fleuve alangui roule des flots de plomb;
Du zénith aveuglant le jour tombe d'aplomb,
Et l'implacable Phré couvre l'Egypte entière.   4

Les grands sphinx qui jamais n'ont baissé la paupière,
Allongés sur leur flanc que baigne un sable blond,
Poursuivent d'un regard mystérieux et long
L'élan démesuré des aiguilles de pierre.   8

Seul, tachant d'un point noir le ciel blanc et serein,
Au loin, tourne sans fin le vol des gypaëtes;
La flamme immense endort les hommes et les bêtes.

Le sol ardent pétille, et l'Anubis d'airain   12
Immobile au milieu de cette chaude joie
Silencieusement vers le soleil aboie.

II

La lune sur le Nil, splendide et ronde, luit.
Et voici que s'émeut la nécropole antique,
Où chaque roi, gardant la pose hiératique,
Gît sous la bandelette et le funèbre enduit.   4

Tel qu'aux jours des Rhamsès, innombrable et sans bruit,
Tout un peuple, formant le cortège mystique,
Multitude qu'absorbe un calme granitique,
S'ordonne et se déploie et marche dans la nuit.   8

Se détachant des murs brodés d'hiéroglyphes,
Ils suivent la Bari que portent les pontifes
D'Ammon-Ra, le grand Dieu conducteur du soleil;

Et les sphinx, les béliers ceints du disque vermeil,   12
Eblouis, d'un seul coup se dressant sur leurs griffes,
S'éveillent en sursaut de l'éternel sommeil.

III

Et la foule grandit plus innombrable encor.
Et le sombre hypogée où s'alignent les couches
Est vide. Du milieu déserté des cartouches,
Les éperviers sacrés ont repris leur essor.   4

Bêtes, peuples et rois, ils vont. L'uræus d'or
S'enroule, étincelant, autour des fronts farouches;
Mais le bitume épais scelle les maigres bouches.
En tête, les grands dieux: Hor, Khnoum, Ptah, Neith, Hathor.   8

Puis tous ceux que conduit Toth Ibiocéphale,
Vêtus de la schenti, coiffés du pschent, ornés
Du lotus bleu. La pompe errante et triomphale

Ondule dans l'horreur des temples ruinés,   12
Et la lune, éclatant au pavé froid des salles,
Prolonge étrangement des ombres colossales.

Le Prisonnier

A Gérôme.

Là-bas, les muezzins ont cessé leurs clameurs.
Le ciel vert, au couchant, de pourpre et d'or se frange;
Le crocodile plonge et cherche un lit de fange,
Et le grand fleuve endort ses dernières rumeurs.   4

Assis, jambes en croix, comme il sied aux fumeurs,
Le Chef rêvait, bercé par le haschisch étrange,
Tandis qu'avec effort faisant mouvoir la cange,
Deux nègres se courbaient, nus, au banc des rameurs.   8

A l'arrière, joyeux et l'insulte à la bouche,
Grattant l'aigre guzla qui rhythme un air farouche,
Se penchait un Arnaute à l'œil féroce et vil;

Car lié sur la barque et saignant sous l'entrave,   12
Un vieux Scheikh regardait d'un air stupide et grave
Les minarets pointus qui tremblent dans le Nil.

Le Samouraï

D'un doigt distrait frôlant la sonore bîva,
A travers les bambous tressés en fine latte,
Elle a vu, par la plage éblouissante et plate,
S'avancer le vainqueur que son amour rêva.   4

C'est lui. Sabres au flanc, l'éventail haut, il va.
La cordelière rouge et le gland écarlate
Coupent l'armure sombre, et, sur l'épaule, éclate
Le blason de Hizen ou de Tokungawa.   8

Ce beau guerrier vêtu de lames et de plaques,
Sous le bronze, la soie et les brillantes laques,
Semble un crustacé noir, gigantesque et vermeil.

Il l'a vue. Il sourit dans la barbe du masque,   12
Et son pas plus hâtif fait reluire au soleil
Les deux antennes d'or qui tremblent à son casque.

Le Daïmio

Sous le noir fouet de guerre à quadruple pompon,
L'étalon belliqueux en hennissant se cabre
Et fait bruire, avec des cliquetis de sabre,
La cuirasse de bronze aux lames du jupon.   4

Le Chef vêtu d'airain, de laque et de crépon,
Otant le masque à poils de son visage glabre,
Regarde le volcan sur un ciel de cinabre
Dresser la neige où rit l'aurore du Nippon.   8

Mais il a vu, vers l'Est éclaboussé d'or, l'astre,
Glorieux d'éclairer ce matin de désastre,
Poindre, orbe éblouissant, au-dessus de la mer;

Et pour couvrir ses yeux dont pas un cil ne bouge,   12
Il ouvre d'un seul coup son éventail de fer
Où dans le satin blanc se lève un Soleil rouge.

Fleurs de feu

Bien des siècles depuis les siècles du Chaos,
La flamme par torrents jaillit de ce cratère,
Et le panache igné du volcan solitaire
Flamba plus haut encor que les Chimborazos.   4

Nul bruit n'éveille plus la cime sans échos.
Où la cendre pleuvait l'oiseau se désaltère;
Le sol est immobile et le sang de la Terre,
La lave, en se figeant, lui laissa le repos.   8

Pourtant, suprême effort de l'antique incendie,
A l'orle de la gueule à jamais refroidie,
Eclatant à travers les rocs pulvérisés,

Comme un coup de tonnerre au milieu du silence,   12
Dans le poudroîment d'or du pollen qu'elle lance,
S'épanouit la fleur des cactus embrasés.

Fleur séculaire

Sur le roc calciné de la dernière rampe
Où le flux volcanique autrefois s'est tari,
La graine que le vent au haut Gualatieri
Sema, germe, s'accroche et, frêle plante, rampe.　　4

Elle grandit. En l'ombre où sa racine trempe,
Son tronc, buvant la flamme obscure, s'est nourri;
Et les soleils d'un siècle ont longuement mûri
Le bouton colossal qui fait ployer sa hampe.　　8

Enfin, dans l'air brûlant et qu'il embrase encor,
Sous le pistil géant qui s'érige, il éclate,
Et l'étamine lance au loin le pollen d'or;

Et le grand aloès à la fleur écarlate,　　12
Pour l'hymen ignoré qu'a rêvé son amour,
Ayant vécu cent ans, n'a fleuri qu'un seul jour.

Le Récif de corail

Le soleil sous la mer, mystérieuse aurore,
Eclaire la forêt des coraux abyssins
Qui mêle, aux profondeurs de ses tièdes bassins,
La bête épanouie et la vivante flore.　　4

Et tout ce que le sel ou l'iode colore,
Mousse, algue chevelue, anémones, oursins,
Couvre de pourpre sombre, en somptueux dessins,
Le fond vermiculé du pâle madrépore.　　8

De sa splendide écaille éteignant les émaux,
Un grand poisson navigue à travers les rameaux;
Dans l'ombre transparente indolemment il rôde;

Et, brusquement, d'un coup de sa nageoire en feu　　12
Il fait, par le cristal morne, immobile et bleu,
Courir un frisson d'or, de nacre et d'émeraude.

LA NATURE ET LE REVE

Médaille antique

L'Etna mûrit toujours la pourpre et l'or du vin
Dont l'Erigone antique enivra Théocrite,
Mais celles dont la grâce en ses vers fut écrite,
Le poète aujourd'hui les chercherait en vain.   4

Perdant la pureté de son profil divin,
Tour à tour Aréthuse esclave et favorite
A mêlé dans sa veine où le sang grec s'irrite
La fureur sarrazine à l'orgueil angevin.   8

Le temps passe. Tout meurt. Le marbre même s'use.
Agrigente n'est plus qu'une ombre, et Syracuse
Dort sous le bleu linceul de son ciel indulgent;

Et seul le dur métal que l'amour fit docile   12
Garde encore en sa fleur, aux médailles d'argent,
L'immortelle beauté des vierges de Sicile.

Les Funérailles

Vers la Phocide illustre, aux temples que domine
La rocheuse Pytho toujours ceinte d'éclairs,
Quand les guerriers anciens descendaient aux enfers,
La Grèce accompagnait leur image divine.   4

Et leurs Ombres, tandis que la nuit illumine
L'Archipel radieux et les golfes déserts,
Ecoutaient, du sommet des promontoires clairs,
Chanter sur leurs tombeaux la mer de Salamine.   8

Et moi je m'éteindrai, vieillard, en un long deuil;
Mon corps sera cloué dans un étroit cercueil
Et l'on paîra la terre et le prêtre et les cierges.

Et pourtant j'ai rêvé ce destin glorieux   12
De tomber au soleil ainsi que les aïeux,
Jeune encore et pleuré des héros et des vierges.

Vendange

Les vendangeurs lassés ayant rompu leurs lignes,
Des voix claires sonnaient à l'air vibrant du soir
Et les femmes, en chœur, marchant vers le pressoir,
Mélaient à leurs chansons des appels et des signes.   4

C'est par un ciel pareil, tout blanc du vol des cygnes,
Que, dans Naxos fumant comme un rouge encensoir,
La Bacchanale vit la Crétoise s'asseoir
Auprès du beau Dompteur ivre du sang des vignes.   8

Aujourd'hui, brandissant le thyrse radieux,
Dionysos vainqueur des bêtes et des Dieux
D'un joug enguirlandé n'étreint plus les panthères;

Mais, fille du soleil, l'Automne enlace encor   12
Du pampre ensanglanté des antiques mystères
La noire chevelure et la crinière d'or.

La Sieste

Pas un seul bruit d'insecte ou d'abeille en maraude.
Tout dort sous les grands bois accablés de soleil
Où le feuillage épais tamise un jour pareil
Au velours sombre et doux des mousses d'émeraude.   4

Criblant le dôme obscur, Midi splendide y rôde
Et, sur mes cils mi-clos alanguis de sommeil,
De mille éclairs furtifs forme un réseau vermeil
Qui s'allonge et se croise à travers l'ombre chaude.   8

Vers la gaze de feu que trament les rayons,
Vole le frêle essaim des riches papillons
Qu'enivrent la lumière et le parfum des sèves;

Alors mes doigts tremblants saisissent chaque fil,   12
Et dans les mailles d'or de ce filet subtil,
Chasseur harmonieux, j'emprisonne mes rêves.

LA MER DE BRETAGNE

Un Peintre

A Emmanuel Lansyer.

Il a compris la race antique aux yeux pensifs
Qui foule le sol dur de la terre bretonne,
La lande rase, rose et grise et monotone
Où croulent les manoirs sous le lierre et les ifs.   4

Des hauts talus plantés de hêtres convulsifs,
Il a vu, par les soirs tempêtueux d'automne,
Sombrer le soleil rouge en la mer qui moutonne;
Sa lèvre s'est salée à l'embrun des récifs.   8

Il a peint l'Océan splendide, immense et triste,
Où le nuage laisse un reflet d'améthyste,
L'émeraude écumante et le calme saphir;

Et fixant l'eau, l'air, l'ombre et l'heure insaisissables,   12
Sur une toile étroite il a fait réfléchir
Le ciel occidental dans le miroir des sables.

Bretagne

Pour que le sang joyeux dompte l'esprit morose,
Il faut, tout parfumé du sel des goëmons,
Que le souffle atlantique emplisse tes poumons;
Arvor t'offre ses caps que la mer blanche arrose.   4

L'ajonc fleurit et la bruyère est déjà rose.
La terre des vieux clans, des nains et des démons,
Ami, te garde encor, sur le granit des monts,
L'homme immobile auprès de l'immuable chose.   8

Viens. Partout tu verras, par les landes d'Arèz,
Monter vers le ciel morne, infrangible cyprès,
Le menhir sous lequel gît la cendre du Brave;

Et l'Océan, qui roule en un lit d'algues d'or   12
Is la voluptueuse et la grande Occismor,
Bercera ton cœur triste à son murmure grave.

Floridum Mare

La moisson débordant le plateau diapré
Roule, ondule et déferle au vent frais qui la berce;
Et le profil, au ciel lointain, de quelque herse
Semble un bateau qui tangue et lève un noir beaupré.   4

Et sous mes pieds, la mer, jusqu'au couchant pourpré,
Céruléenne ou rose ou violette ou perse
Ou blanche de moutons que le reflux disperse,
Verdoie à l'infini comme un immense pré.   8

Aussi les goëlands qui suivent la marée,
Vers les blés mûrs que gonfle une houle dorée,
Avec des cris joyeux, volaient en tourbillons;

Tandis que, de la terre, une brise emmiellée   12
Eparpillait au gré de leur ivresse ailée
Sur l'Océan fleuri des vols de papillons.

Soleil couchant

Les ajoncs éclatants, parure du granit,
Dorent l'âpre sommet que le couchant allume;
Au loin, brillante encor par sa barre d'écume,
La mer sans fin commence où la terre finit.   4

A mes pieds, c'est la nuit, le silence. Le nid
Se tait, l'homme est rentré sous le chaume qui fume;
Seul, l'Angélus du soir, ébranlé dans la brume,
A la vaste rumeur de l'Océan s'unit.   8

Alors, comme du fond d'un abîme, des traînes,
Des landes, des ravins, montent des voix lointaines
De pâtres attardés ramenant le bétail.

L'horizon tout entier s'enveloppe dans l'ombre,   12
Et le soleil mourant, sur un ciel riche et sombre,
Ferme les branches d'or de son rouge éventail.

Maris Stella

Sous les coiffes de lin, toutes, croisant leurs bras
Vêtus de laine rude ou de mince percale,
Les femmes, à genoux sur le roc de la cale,
Regardent l'Océan blanchir l'île de Batz.   4

Les hommes, pères, fils, maris, amants, là-bas,
Avec ceux de Paimpol, d'Audierne et de Cancale,
Vers le Nord, sont partis pour la lointaine escale.
Que de hardis pêcheurs qui ne reviendront pas!   8

Par-dessus la rumeur de la mer et des côtes
Le chant plaintif s'élève, invoquant à voix hautes
L'Etoile sainte, espoir des marins en péril;

Et l'Angélus, courbant tous ces fronts noirs de hâle,   12
Des clochers de Roscoff à ceux de Sybiril
S'envole, tinte et meurt dans le ciel rose et pâle.

Le Bain

L'homme et la bête, tels que le beau monstre antique,
Sont entrés dans la mer, et nus, libres, sans frein,
Parmi la brume d'or de l'âcre pulvérin,
Sur le ciel embrasé font un groupe athlétique.   4

Et l'étalon sauvage et le dompteur rustique,
Humant à pleins poumons l'odeur du sel marin,
Se plaisent à laisser sur la chair et le crin
Frémir le flot glacé de la rude Atlantique.   8

La houle s'enfle, court, se dresse comme un mur
Et déferle. Lui crie. Il hennit, et sa queue
En jets éblouissants fait rejaillir l'eau bleue;

Et, les cheveux épars, s'effarant dans l'azur,   12
Ils opposent, cabrés, leur poitrail noir qui fume,
Au for t échevelé de la fumante écume.

Blason céleste

J'ai vu parfois, ayant tout l'azur pour émail,
Les nuages d'argent et de pourpre et de cuivre,
A l'Occident où l'œil s'éblouit à les suivre,
Peindre d'un grand blason le céleste vitrail.   4

Pour cimier, pour supports, l'héraldique bétail,
Licorne, léopard, alérion ou guivre,
Monstres, géants captifs qu'un coup de vent délivre,
Exhaussent leur stature et cabrent leur poitrail.   8

Certe, aux champs de l'espace, en ces combats étranges
Que les noirs Séraphins livrèrent aux Archanges,
Cet écu fut gagné par un Baron du ciel;

Comme ceux qui jadis prirent Constantinople,   12
Il porte, en bon croisé, qu'il soit George ou Michel,
Le soleil, besant d'or, sur la mer de sinople.

Armor

Pour me conduire au Raz, j'avais pris à Trogor
Un berger chevelu comme un ancien Evhage ;
Et nous foulions, humant son arome sauvage,
L'âpre terre kymrique où croît le genêt d'or.   4

Le couchant rougissait et nous marchions encor,
Lorsque le souffle amer me fouetta le visage ;
Et l'homme, par delà le morne paysage
Etendant un long bras, me dit : Senèz Ar-mor !   8

Et je vis, me dressant sur la bruyère rose,
L'Océan qui, splendide et monstrueux, arrose
Du sel vert de ses eaux les caps de granit noir ;

Et mon cœur savoura, devant l'horizon vide   12
Que reculait vers l'Ouest l'ombre immense du soir,
L'ivresse de l'espace et du vent intrépide.

Mer montante

Le soleil semble un phare à feux fixes et blancs.
Du Raz jusqu'à Penmarc'h la côte entière fume,
Et seuls, contre le vent qui rebrousse leur plume,
A travers la tempête errent les goëlands.   4

L'une après l'autre, avec de furieux élans,
Les lames glauques, sous leur crinière d'écume
Dans un tonnerre sourd s'éparpillant en brume,
Empanachent au loin les récifs ruisselants.   8

Et j'ai laissé courir le flot de ma pensée,
Rêves, espoirs, regrets de force dépensée,
Sans qu'il en reste rien qu'un souvenir amer.

L'Océan m'a parlé d'une voix fraternelle,   12
Car la même clameur que pousse encor la mer
Monte de l'homme aux Dieux, vainement éternelle.

Brise marine

L'hiver a défleuri la lande et le courtil.
Tout est mort. Sur la roche uniformément grise
Où la lame sans fin de l'Atlantique brise,
Le pétale fané pend au dernier pistil.   4

Et pourtant je ne sais quel arome subtil
Exhalé de la mer jusqu'à moi par la brise,
D'un effluve si tiède emplit mon cœur qu'il grise ;
Ce souffle étrangement parfumé, d'où vient-il ?   8

Ah ! Je le reconnais. C'est de trois mille lieues
Qu'il vient, de l'Ouest, là-bas où les Antilles bleues
Se pâment sous l'ardeur de l'astre occidental ;

Et j'ai, de ce récif battu du flot kymrique,   12
Respiré dans le vent qu'embauma l'air natal
La fleur jadis éclose au jardin d'Amérique.

La Conque

Par quels froids Océans, depuis combien d'hivers,
—Qui le saura jamais, Conque frêle et nacrée !—
La houle sous-marine et les raz de marée
T'ont-ils roulée au creux de leurs abîmes verts ?   4

Aujourd'hui, sous le ciel, loin des reflux amers,
Tu t'es fait un doux lit de l'arène dorée.
Mais ton espoir est vain. Longue et désespérée,
En toi gémit toujours la grande voix des mers.   8

Mon âme est devenue une prison sonore ;
Et comme en tes replis pleure et soupire encore
La plainte du refrain de l'ancienne clameur ;

Ainsi du plus profond de ce cœur trop plein d'Elle,   12
Sourde, lente, insensible et pourtant éternelle,
Gronde en moi l'orageuse et lointaine rumeur.

Le Lit

Qu'il soit encourtiné de brocart ou de serge,
Triste comme une tombe ou joyeux comme un nid,
C'est là que l'homme naît, se repose et s'unit,
Enfant, époux, vieillard, aïeule, femme ou vierge.   4

Funèbre ou nuptial, que l'eau sainte l'asperge
Sous le noir crucifix ou le rameau bénit,
C'est là que tout commence et là que tout finit,
De la première aurore au feu du dernier cierge.   8

Humble, rustique et clos, ou fier du pavillon
Triomphalement peint d'or et de vermillon,
Qu'il soit de chêne brut, de cyprès ou d'érable;

Heureux qui peut dormir sans peur et sans remords   12
Dans le lit paternel, massif et vénérable,
Où tous les siens sont nés aussi bien qu'ils sont morts.

La Mort de l'Aigle

Quand l'aigle a dépassé les neiges éternelles,
A ses larges poumons il veut chercher plus d'air
Et le soleil plus proche en un azur plus clair
Pour échauffer l'éclat de ses mornes prunelles.   4

Il s'enlève. Il aspire un torrent d'étincelles.
Toujours plus haut, enflant son vol tranquille et fier,
Il plane sur l'orage et monte vers l'éclair;
Mais la foudre d'un coup a rompu ses deux ailes.   8

Avec un cri sinistre, il tournoie, emporté
Par la trombe, et, crispé, buvant d'un trait sublime
La flamme éparse, il plonge au fulgurant abîme.

Heureux qui pour la Gloire ou pour la Liberté,   12
Dans l'orgueil de la force et l'ivresse du rêve,
Meurt ainsi, d'une mort éblouissante et brève!

Plus Ultra

L'homme a conquis la terre ardente des lions
Et celle des venins et celle des reptiles,
Et troublé l'Océan où cinglent les nautiles
Du sillage doré des anciens galions.   4

Mais plus loin que la neige et que les tourbillons
Du Ström et que l'horreur des Spitzbergs infertiles,
Le Pôle bat d'un flot tiède et libre des îles
Où nul marin n'a pu hisser ses pavillons.   8

Partons! Je briserai l'infranchissable glace,
Car dans mon corps hardi je porte une âme lasse
Du facile renom des conquérants de l'or.

J'irai. Je veux monter au dernier promontoire,   12
Et qu'une mer, pour tous silencieuse encor,
Caresse mon orgueil d'un murmure de gloire.

La Vie des Morts

Au poète Armand Silvestre.

Lorsque la sombre croix sur nous sera plantée,
La terre nous ayant tous deux ensevelis,
Ton corps refleurira dans la neige des lys
Et de ma chair naîtra la rose ensanglantée.   4

Et la divine Mort que tes vers ont chantée,
En son vol noir chargé de silence et d'oublis,
Nous fera par le ciel, bercés d'un lent roulis,
Vers des astres nouveaux une route enchantée.   8

Et montant au soleil, en son vivant foyer,
Nos deux esprits iront se fondre et se noyer
Dans la félicité des flammes éternelles;

Cependant que sacrant le poète et l'ami,   1
La Gloire nous fera vivre à jamais parmi
Les Ombres que la Lyre a faites fraternelles.

Au Tragédien E. Rossi

APRES UNE RECITATION DE DANTE

O Rossi, je t'ai vu, traînant le manteau noir,
Briser le faible cœur de la triste Ophélie,
Et, tigre exaspéré d'amour et de folie,
Etrangler tes sanglots dans le fatal mouchoir.   4

J'ai vu Lear et Macbeth et pleuré de te voir
Baiser, suprême amant de l'antique Italie,
Au tombeau nuptial Juliette pâlie.
Pourtant tu fus plus grand et plus terrible, un soir.   8

Car j'ai goûté l'horreur et le plaisir sublimes,
Pour la première fois, d'entendre les trois rimes
Sonner par ta voix d'or leur fanfare de fer;

Et, rouge du reflet de l'infernale flamme,   12
J'ai vu—j'en ai frémi jusques au fond de l'âme—
Alighieri vivant dire un chant de l'Enfer.

Michel-Ange

Certe, il était hanté d'un tragique tourment,
Alors qu'à la Sixtine et loin de Rome en fêtes,
Solitaire, il peignait Sibylles et Prophètes,
Et, sur le sombre mur, le dernier Jugement.   4

Il écoutait en lui pleurer obstinément,
Titan que son désir enchaîne aux plus hauts faîtes,
La Patrie et l'Amour, la Gloire et leurs défaites;
Il songeait que tout meurt et que le rêve ment.   8

Aussi ces lourds Géants, las de leur force exsangue,
Ces Esclaves qu'étreint une infrangible gangue,
Comme il les a tordus d'une étrange façon;

Et dans les marbres froids où bout son âme altière,   12
Comme il a fait courir avec un grand frisson
La colère d'un Dieu vaincu par la Matière!

Sur un Marbre brisé

La mousse fut pieuse en fermant ses yeux mornes;
Car, dans ce bois inculte, il chercherait en vain
La Vierge qui versait le lait pur et le vin
Sur la terre au beau nom dont il marqua les bornes.　　4

Aujourd'hui le houblon, le lierre et les viornes
Qui s'enroulent autour de ce débris divin,
Ignorant s'il fut Pan, Faune, Hermès ou Silvain,
A son front mutilé tordent leurs vertes cornes.　　8

Vois. L'oblique rayon, le caressant encor,
Dans sa face camuse a mis deux orbes d'or;
La vigne folle y rit comme une lèvre rouge;

Et, prestige mobile, un murmure du vent,　　12
Les feuilles, l'ombre errante et le soleil qui bouge,
De ce marbre en ruine ont fait un Dieu vivant.

COMMENTARIES

The text is that of the first edition of *Les Trophées*, Lemerre, 1893 (but see the note at the end of my Introduction). There is one sonnet, now famous, which was first published in *La Nouvelle Revue* on 15 February 1893, 'Le Thermodon':

> Vers Thémiscyre en feu qui tout le jour trembla
> Des clameurs et du choc de la cavalerie,
> Dans l'ombre, morne et lent, le Thermodon charrie
> Cadavres, armes, chars que la mort y roula.
>
> Où sont Marpé, Phœbé, Philippis, Aella,
> Qui, suivant Hippolyte et l'ardente Astérie,
> Menèrent l'escadron royal à la tuerie ?
> Leurs corps déchevelés et blêmes gisent là.
>
> Telle une floraison de lys géants fauchée,
> La rive est aux deux bords de guerrières jonchée
> Où, parfois, se débat et hennit un cheval ;
>
> Et l'Euxin vit, à l'aube, aux plus lointaines berges
> Du fleuve ensanglanté d'amont jusqu'en aval,
> Fuir des étalons blancs rouges du sang des Vierges.

The sonnet did not appear in the original edition of *Les Trophées* on 16 February 1893 but was put in the section 'La Grèce et la Sicile', between 'Jason et Médée' and 'Artémis', in the duodecimo edition of May 1893. It has kept this position in subsequent editions of *Les Trophées*. The fifth line was later changed to 'Où sont Phœbé, Marpé, Philippis, Aella'.

I give at the beginning of each commentary the date and place of only the first publication of each sonnet. For details of their frequent publication at other times, one should consult Ibrovac's chronological list of the poems: *José-Maria de Heredia, sa vie—son œuvre*, ii, pp. 583–94. It is not the policy of this series to give the variant readings of the poems, save for some exceptional points of interest. All variants of *Les Trophées*, all Heredia's sonnets not published in this collection as well as all his other published poetry, can be found in *Poésies complètes de Heredia, Les Trophées, Sonnets et Poèmes divers, Texte définitif avec notes et variantes*, Lemerre, 1924. Useful notes, in Spanish, can be found in two Spanish translations of Heredia's collection, one by Max Henriquez Ureña (*Los Trofeos (Sonetos)*, 1954), the other by José Antonio Niño (*Los Trofeos*, 1957). Further details of works on Heredia can be found in the monograph in our series: the most complete source is Ibrovac (in addition to the two volumes to which frequent reference is made, there is the comprehensive third volume: *Les Sources des 'Trophées'*).

Very important in *Les Trophées* are what some call sound effects, that is, euphony, harmony, alliteration, assonance, viz. Heredia's sonorous use of language. Theorists like Maurice Grammont (*Le Vers français: ses moyens d'expression, son harmonie,*) believe that certain sounds necessarily help to create certain effects and meanings, provided that the sense of the words goes in the same direction. Grammont includes many illustrations from *Les Trophées* and his comments can be very illuminating. But his approach presents dangers, especially that of finding too much 'imitative harmony', viz. cases where the sound is alleged to echo the sense. This certainly occurs but the harmony is often better seen, not as imitative but rather as self-sufficient, the autonomous pleasure in associations of sound, rhythm and meaning. The matter is exceedingly complex both in theory and in practice: we would need a volume of many hundreds of pages to analyse the harmony of every poem in Heredia's collection. Some sonnets or parts of sonnets will be carefully examined but the reader must be left to pursue on his own the many details involved in these aspects of Heredia's art; many readers are content to be affected by them and to enjoy limited consciousness of their beauty without attempting the close analysis which certainly sharpens our appreciation.

A LECONTE DE LISLE

The 'sacred memory' recalled in the Preface's first paragraph and which had to take precedence over Leconte de Lisle for the book's dedication was, of course, that of Heredia's mother (see p. 30). But this Preface really amounts to a dedication. Already a keen admirer of the older poet's work, Heredia first came to know him personally in 1863, that is, in Heredia's twenty-first year. They became very close personal friends, regularly consulting each other about the poems they were writing. Leconte de Lisle's example, encouragement and advice were invaluable to Heredia who showed deep love and respect for what he and many poets of his time saw as the noble devotion to art and craftsmanship shown by the Master.

LA GRECE ET LA SICILE

See the Introduction, p. 6.

L'Oubli
La République des lettres, 16 July 1876 (with the title 'En Campanie')
This sonnet systematically exploits concrete detail and telling antithesis. The first quatrain depicts the ruined temple on the lonely promontory,

contrasting former glories with present decay. The second quatrain is entirely devoted to the herdsman: the scene's desolation is emphasized by the fact that he comes here only occasionally, and then alone. Behind the solitary figure of the herdsman standing out, by both shape and colour, against the vast expanse of calm blue sky, the background is felt to be infinity, and infinity is almost the poet's viewpoint. A gentle, mournful sadness is conveyed by the quiet resignation of the sense and by the muted music of the verse (the repeated *b*s of *bouvier*, *buffle*, *boire*, the repetition in '*où soupire*', the drawn-out sounds of *conque*, *soupire*, *azur*, *noir*, all stressed syllables). Earth is kind to these ruins which experience a form of rebirth in Heredia's poetic conceit as the sculptured acanthus leaf on the fallen pillar is depicted as growing green each year. But modern man has forgotten the past legends and dreams; he hears but does not understand or respond to the sea's lament over the Sirens who drowned themselves because of Ulysses's indifference to their singing, he is indifferent to the suggestion that Heredia puts into 'du fond des nuits sereines'. Here, as so often in Heredia's sonnets, the quatrains provide a background of detail for the tercets' significant conclusion. The capital letters, of which there is an unusually high number—*Mort, Déesses, Héros, Terre, Dieux, Homme, Mer, Sirènes*—are doubtless meant to convey the words' symbolic force.

The last line of the sonnet is climactic not just by sense but by density of alliteration and assonance. Grammont (p. 219) gives a good example of arbitrarily subjective interpretation of the line's sounds: '*a è i*—la vague commence à s'élever, *è a an é an*—la vague gronde, *é i è*—la vague meurt sur la rive'.

HERCULE ET LES CENTAURES

Némée

La Jeune France, July 1884

Heredia's grandiosely fierce sonnet recalls one of the twelve tasks which fell to Hercules ('le Dompteur'), the killing of the lion that ravaged the inhabitants of Nemea. We do not witness the actual struggle; instead, and more forcefully, the first of the poem's suggestive 'big effects'—the huge print, the lion's roar—work on our imagination, assisted by the dramatic brevity of l. 4. The cleverly composed second quatrain begins to intensify the tone, but still mostly at one remove from the combatants. We are led from the picture of the fleeing, terror-stricken shepherd (and the physiological detail of eyes wide with fear) through his dramatic posture of turning back to see the cause of his horror. The *enjambement* into l. 8 throws appropriate emphasis onto *surgir* which, with the last words of the line, forms an interesting climactic oxymoron, a first and not yet fully intelligible indication of the sight which it is the sestet's function to develop and, in l. 14, fully to explain. In l. 9, the sense of the shepherd's sudden sharp cry is heightened by the dramatic brevity and cogent hiatus (. . . 'cri*e. Il*'). From 'Il a vu' to the end of l. 11 there begins a fresh build-up of detail (the sympathetic horror of the blood-red sunset, the dishevelled mane of the lion and its sinister fangs) which, with menacing force, leads to the definitive climactic oxymoron of the last line ('monstrueux héros'): Hercules is lifting up the slaughtered lion's skin so that man and beast seem one. For both emotional and pictorial effect, Heredia loves to telescope into harsh, vibrant unity such violently opposed impressions, especially, in this subsection, the human and the bestial.

Stymphale

Revue des deux mondes, 15 January 1888

This sonnet forms a diptych with 'Némée'. Another of the legendary hero's tasks was to drive off with his bow and arrows the iron-beaked, sharp-feathered cranes that were plaguing the swampy lake of Stymphalos. Like 'Némée', this poem may owe something to Gustave Moreau's cycle of paintings about Hercules; and, like 'Némée' too, though perhaps not quite so fiercely, 'Stymphale' concentrates heavily, especially in the first tercet, on the spectacle's horror, so that a similarly piquant and climactic fusion of contrasts can be achieved in the last line: blood, smiling face and big blue sky.

6. *Omphale*: queen of Lydia to whom Hercules was sold by Hermes and by whom he was set to do women's work.

Nessus

Revue des deux mondes, 15 January 1888

This is the Nessus who fell in love with Deianeira, wife of Hercules (l. 9, 'l'Epouse triomphale'), tried to molest her and was killed by Hercules. Nessus is one of the Centaurs, fabulous monsters half-men, half-horses, who lived in Thessaly. Heredia shows Nessus painfully emerging from the purely animal state through love of a woman to something approaching a more complex human level of experience. The sonnet gains greater animation through direct address, including imprecation, and the strong opposition between the octet and the sestet. Before seeing Deianeira, Nessus lived a happy and heedless animal existence: he roamed far and wide and knew the clean physical exuberance of dashing through ice-cold mountain streams (note too the colour contrast of water on bright red hair). The theme of the carefree, vigorous life is concisely summarized in the fifth line, packed with telling adjectives. The smell of the mares, the female Centaurs, in heat, was a slightly discordant note in his carefree virile happiness (and anticipates the brutal lust depicted later) but it was not truly discordant since it was a purely bestial desire. Seeing Deianeira in Hercules's arms (note the 'spiritual', specifically human, quality implied by *sourire*) has given him a lust more powerful than ever and nearer to human love because it remains an unsatisfied yearning (cf. the strong physiological detail of bristling hair in l. 11, intensified by the insistent, harsh *s* sounds, the *i*'s of 'désir' and 'hérisse' and the harsh hiatus of 'm*e* harcèle' and '*et hé*risse'). The last line is as climactically summary as any in *Les Trophées*, by the energetic juxtaposition of all-conquering lust and love, each occupying a hemistich and each hemistich symmetrically divided 2/4: *rut* and *étalon* are nicely contrasted, yet also fused, with *amour* and *l'homme*. The almost thumping rhythm emphasizes these four words and also *dompte*. There are first the sharp stabs of the two short-syllabled words *rut* and *étalon*, followed by two much longer nasal syllables in *amour* and *dompte* (suggesting more protracted yearning?) and, with the short syllable *l'homme*, the line ends as stabbingly as it began.

La Centauresse
Revue des deux mondes, 15 January 1888

This sonnet forms a diptych with 'Nessus', depicting the nostalgic sadness of the female Centaur abandoned by the males who, like Nessus, are trying to rise above their animality by seeking union with women. Less harshly intense in tone than 'Nessus', 'La Centauresse' nevertheless has much in common with it, in general theme and even at similar points (e.g. the colour contrast again in l. 4, the suggestive bestial lust in ll. 7 and 8). As in 'Nessus', the second tercet compactly and evocatively sums up the poem's theme.

10. Ixion tried to seduce Hera; she complained to Zeus, who formed a double of her, Nephele, from a cloud (as the Greek name implies). By Nephele, Ixion became the father of the race of Centaurs.

Centaures et Lapithes
Revue des deux mondes, 15 January 1888

The scene is the wedding of Hippodamia (l. 5, 'L'Epouse polluée') and Pirithoüs (Thessalian hero, son of Ixion and king of the Lapiths). The Lapiths were mythological people of Thessaly, great tamers of horses; they fought the Centaurs (l. 4, 'fils de la Nuée'—see end of commentary on 'La Centauresse') who had come to abduct Hippodamia and who insulted the women there. Vianey interprets Hercules routing the Centaurs as the sun chasing away the storm demons. The theme is dramatic enough in itself; Heredia heightens the drama by his sonorous language (especially in ll. 6–8 and 13–14) and his construction: the octet describes a general scene of violence which gives place to a typical close-up, awesomely intense in the contained dynamism of its climax, of Hercules's terrible eye cowing the retreating Centaurs. The last line, powerful in its sense and sound effects, especially the repeated *s*s, is characteristically well prepared: Hercules's strength and size are described before he is identified and l. 12 gives a dramatic background of space and depth.

Fuite de Centaures
Revue des deux mondes, 15 January 1888

This sonnet forms a diptych with 'Centaures et Lapithes'. Routed by Hercules, the Centaurs flee towards Ossa (a mountain in Thessaly), Olympus (the famous mountain home of the gods, between Macedonia and Thessaly) and Pelion (a chain of mountains in Thessaly, between the gulf of Magnesia and the Aegean sea. On its north side, it joins up with Ossa). Again, we may note Heredia's technique, in the octet, of giving the background (flight through the thickets and waterfalls amidst the mountains): the tone is urgent (with a characteristically bestial, olfactory impression in ll. 3–4) but not very intense. The highest point of intensity comes in the last line, with the menacingly huge and sombre shadow of the pursuing Hercules, which is the reason for the Centaurs' flight and is typically and dramatically kept for the end of the poem. The sestet builds up to this point in a manner recalling the sestet in 'Némée'.

3. *La peur les précipite*: the second hemistich of a line from Théramène's famous *récit* near the end of Racine's *Phèdre*.

La Naissance d'Aphrodite
Unpublished before *Les Trophées*, 1893

Thauziès and Ibrovac both think this poem is rather obscure, mostly because Heredia has tried to say too many things at once. His aim is to link the origins of the world with the birth of beauty and love. According to the Ancients, Chaos was the infinite space before creation, a confused mixture of all the elements before the gods gave them their place and order. The Greeks made Chaos the oldest divinity. The Titans were mythological beings who inhabited the sky; they were the sons of Ouranos (Sky) and Gaia (Earth—'Gaia à la large poitrine' as she was described by Ménard, following Hesiod, in his *Du Polythéisme hellénique*). Ouranos, first sovereign of the universe, threw his sons into Tartarus (viz. Hell—cf. l. 5: the Styx is Hell's river). Gaia, indignant, counselled her sons to rise against their father and gave one son, Cronos, a diamond sickle with which he mutilated his father Ouranos, then dethroned him and took possession of Heaven. From the blood which, as Ouranos was castrated, fell into and mingled with the sea, Aphrodite (the Greek Venus) was born.

The second quatrain may be intended to recall the troubled period between the downfall of the Titans and the coming of Zeus. The rhymes of the last four lines are especially interesting. Throughout *Les Trophées* Heredia scrupulously adheres to the classical *alternance des rimes*. Though, technically speaking, the last four lines here are no exception, one notes that they all have the same sound and are really, for the ear, masculine rhymes.

Jason et Médée
La Renaissance littéraire et artistique, 28 September 1872

This poem was inspired by Moreau's painting on the same theme (hence the dedication: see Ibrovac, ii, pp. 345-6, for a careful comparison of painting and poem); it evokes an atmosphere of heavily exotic bewitchment and insidious threat. Jason, leader of the legendary Argonautic expedition to recover the Golden Fleece, was helped by Medea (second daughter of Aietes, king of Colchis, where the Fleece was kept) to perform the tasks required of him by Aietes in exchange for the Fleece (l. 8). Medea helped Jason because the goddess Hera had made her fall in love with him. In a forceful contrast with present happiness, ll. 13-14 suggest Medea's origins (she was an enchantress, a priestess of Hecate), her jealous and passionate nature and the tragic future that lay in store for their love.

  · 1. Grammont (p. 282) argues that the many nasals help to suggest 'la lenteur, la langueur, la mollesse, la nonchalance'.

  7. *Le Héros* is, of course, Jason and, l. 12, *la fatale Epouse* Medea.

ARTEMIS ET LES NYMPHES

Artémis
Le Parnasse contemporain, 1866

This sonnet forms a triptych with 'La Chasse' and 'Nymphée'. The Greek goddess Artemis is the Roman Diana, associated with wild life and hunting, with the young of all living things, with child-birth and hence with the moon. Heredia's poem sees her as the virgin huntress. The shafts from her bow are moonbeams. Her father, Jupiter, granted her request that she should never marry. He gave her arrows and a company of nymphs, making her queen of the woods. Heredia animates further an already vivid subject by a favourite device, apostrophe, as he communicates the sexless, or perhaps more properly, the virile Artemis's muscular exultation in the wild life of the woods, in hunting and killing, smelling the forest smells and, in the sestet, even enjoying the very pain which the tracked animal inflicts on the hunter when it attacks and bites her before being killed.

  The first quatrain is descriptive, dynamic and kinaesthetic, with its emphasis on Artemis's eager inhalation of the bitter, pungent smells of the forest (an aspect of her sensuality which is never channelled into normal sexual love) and, in l. 4, on a characteristic gesture—throwing back her hair—a significant detail of the busy extrovert intent on the hunt. The *coupe* at the end of l. 4, the position of 'tu pars!', help to convey the sense of Artemis's bound into action. In l. 3, 'virginale et virile' form a striking oxymoron: the line's vigour is reinforced by the repeated *v*s and *is*. In the second quatrain, Artemis's dogs (*léopards*) give more detail to suggest violence and ferocity (cf. the repeated *r*s): the roaring is amplified by reverberation in both space and time. In ll. 7–8, the reiterated emphasis on the goddess's deft quickness leads to the condensed violence of a typical Heredia blood-bath. The climax of the sestet explores a less conventional, more disturbingly subtle and strange aspect of Artemis's open-air sensuality: something approaching masochism (cf. l. 12 and the oxymoron 'douceur cruelle'). She exults in exertion, even in pain, because it intensifies her sense of physical well-being, of existing primarily through the senses. Line 14 is a more excitingly horrible and intense blood-bath than the one in l. 8.

La Chasse
Le Parnasse contemporain, 1866

The first two quatrains, describing the ascent of Phoebus Apollo's four-horse chariot (viz. the growing strength of the sun's light), are a fairly quiet background for the violent introduction, in the sestet, of Artemis, whose actual name is dramatically held back until the last line and whose activity, appearance and nature strongly recall the previous poem.

It is interesting to compare the second quatrain of this sonnet with the 1866 version: a few changes (cf. the words italicised below) enable Heredia to make it rather more dramatic:

> *La lumière filtrant sous les feuillages* lents,
> Dans l'ombre où rit le timbre des fontaines,
> *Fait trembler* à travers les cimes incertaines,
> *Au caprice du vent*, ses jeux étincelants.

Nymphée
La Vie moderne, 3 July 1879

For the various modifications this poem underwent, see *Poésies complètes de Heredia*, pp. 208–9. Cf. Bibliography. The octet describes the descent of the chariot conducted by Phoebus Apollo, the Sun-God (cf. l. 3: 'Le Dieu'), that is, sunset and the quiet fall of evening so often treated in Heredia's sonnets. 'Nymphée' completes Phoebus Apollo's journey and in the tercets, characteristically more dramatic than the octet, gives a last mention of Artemis and suggestively introduces Pan; it is, then, a kind of bridge between the two previous sonnets and the two that follow. Ibrovac sees 'Nymphée' as influenced by the painter Gustave Moreau; Ureña (p. 148) seems nearer the truth when he suggests Corot (cf. the quiet radiance and colour exhaled in the second quatrain).

8. The four repeated nasal vowels evoke silence, according to Grammont (p. 286). Their repetition is certainly pleasurable in itself.

13. The five sounds in *an* or *en* suggest, according to Grammont (p. 217), 'mouvement ou bruit répété indéfiniment'.

Pan
La Revue française, 1 May 1863

This sonnet forms a diptych with 'Le Bain des nymphes'. Pan had the horns, ears and legs of a goat (cf. l. 3: 'Le Chèvre-pied'). His character too was goatish: as here depicted, he was lustful and playful. Like nearly all Heredia's sonnets about ancient Greece, 'Pan' is very dramatic in theme and treatment: the silence of the forest envelops both Pan and the nymph, who are strongly contrasted as the one stalks silently with burning eye and the other, losing her way, surrenders with innocent joy to the ambient freshness and musical ploppings of the dripping trees. Our interest is held in suspense until the sudden fierce climax in the second tercet. Heredia thus emphasizes the speed of the seizure and of the forest's return to silence.

Le Bain des nymphes
Revue des deux mondes, 15 May 1890 (with the title: 'Nymphée')

The first two lines situate the landscape, the description of the nymphs in the rest of the octet reveals a discreet, purely pictorial sensuality, establishing the background for the contrasting irruption of Pan (l. 11, 'le Satyre'). Typically, Heredia gives the succinctly threatening description of Pan (l. 10) before he actually names him.

1. 'l'Euxin': Pontus Euxinus, the Black Sea.

14. The Caistro was a small river in Asia Minor famous for its swans.

Le Vase
L'Artiste, 1 February 1868

By a characteristic bringing together of the small and the large, one vase or goblet here serves to evoke various Greek legends: Jason and Medea (see 'Jason et Médée'), the Bacchantes, priestesses and followers of Bacchus drunk with wine (l. 6: 'ivres du doux poison') as they bedeck the bulls that went in their procession, the clash of arms which is immediately contrasted with a more quietly and resonantly sad perspective of eternal mourning and, final suggestively sensual climax, the Chimeras on the two handles of the cup. The Chimera was a fire-breathing monster shaped like a lion in front, a dragon behind and a goat in the middle. For Grammont (pp. 229–30), the repeated *en* or *an* sounds in ll. 7–8 and l. 12 are bad because they do not accord with the ideas expressed. It can be claimed that the repetitions are pleasurable in themselves and/or that they help to evoke an impression of extended pleasure.

Ariane

Le Siècle littéraire, 1 January 1876 (earliest version, very different, published as 'Le Triomphe d'Iacchos' in *La Revue française*, 1 May 1863)

Iacchos or Bacchus was the god of wine and the symbol of nature's wild fertility: he was usually followed by a revel-rout and his conquests (cf. l. 14) extended to India and Asia. 'L'infidèle amant' of l. 13 is Theseus, who after using the enamoured Ariadne's assistance against the Cretan Minotaur abandoned her in Naxos. Ariadne's relations with these two lovers have been treated by many painters, sculptors and poets. The sonnet is compactly exotic and voluptuous. The brass cymbals in l. 1 begin to create the wildly sonorous context of the Bacchanalian orgy sustained by the resonant rhymes and, with undertones of harsh ferocity, by the *r* sounds repeated throughout the poem. The specifically lustful atmosphere is of course inherent in the Bacchanalian orgy: Heredia intensifies this atmosphere by the piquant placing of the bare Ariadne on a tiger that is seen as responding with raucous desire to its voluptuous burden and to the sensitive touches of her hand. Having thus excited our interest in the octet by the desire beneath Ariadne, Heredia briefly, in the first tercet, reinforces his picture with three further details—the flowing hair, the arched flank and the black grapes—and then ends with a further prolongation of his theme of lust. The prolongation entails a variation that is, so to speak, both physical or positional (the desire is no longer below but out and away from Ariadne, coming from and directed towards the advancing Bacchus) and psychological (the purely bestial overtone is dropped: Ariadne welcomes the threatening eroticism of the all-conquering Bacchus).

Bacchanale

Le Parnasse contemporain, 1876

The sonnet has much in common with the previous one: the concentration is even greater on the wildness of the Bacchanalian orgy. The repeated *r* sounds have a similar function; many of the rhymes are again resonant. The poem is a brilliant exercise in the mounting effects—pictorial, colourful and sonorous—of animality, ferocity and brutal ecstasy. In l. 11 we find adumbrated the threat of an orgy of blood for the roaming tigers. Here, as in 'Ariane' or 'Némée', the presence of the animals is very important for the picturesquely harsh, vibrant effects Heredia can achieve through the interfusion of the human and the bestial. The most intense point, as one might expect, comes in the climactic second tercet as Bacchus, waving his wand (*thyrse*), exhorts the company to sexual excesses, especially in the stridently bestial last line. Interestingly, the 1876 version of this last line: 'Le mâle rugissant à la blanche femelle' offered both a measure of fierce sound and an implicit colour contrast (suggesting the white helplessness of the female?) but the latter was sacrificed to repeat and hence augment the stridency.

10. Grammont (p. 272) notes the sombre vowels ('gr*ond*ements . . . pro*long*e . . . l*ong*') which give a 'grondement sourd' (p. 299).

Le Réveil d'un Dieu
Le Livre des sonnets, Lemerre, 1874

Heredia gives a synthesis of the spring myth of Adonis (l. 8: 'Le jeune homme', and l. 11, 'L'Epoux mystérieux'), who, in one version of the myth, was loved by Venus and died hunting, gored by a wild boar. Venus obtained permission from Jupiter for Adonis to stay with Proserpine (Queen of the Underworld) only part of the year and the rest with Venus on Olympus. Venus is here called Astarté, the name given to the Phoenician and Syrian divinity, goddess of Heaven, who was equivalent to the Roman Venus Urania and the Greek Aphrodite. In Biblos, city of ancient Phoenicia (and also in Athens and Alexandria), Adonis was especially worshipped. His festivals entailed two ceremonies: mourning at his death, with women weeping and pulling at their hair, followed by games to celebrate his resurrection. From Adonis's blood sprang the rose of the anemone (cf. ll. 13–14). We can thus see the outlines of a myth of the Greek Mother and her lover who dies as the vegetation dies but comes to life again with the spring.

Line 2, like l. 13 of 'Bacchanale', suggests something of an almost Baudelairean delectation in the complex pleasure that can be deliberately sought in grief as well as in the senses. Heredia's sonnet is rather *décadent* in its sophisticated fusion of tones: the scented purity of the funeral in the second quatrain, the *fin de siècle* 'longs yeux languissants' (l. 6), the ecstatic, incantatory lines 11 and 12 which Mallarmé or Valéry would not have disavowed.

La Magicienne
Le Parnasse contemporain, 1876

This sonnet has a Racinian quality, in its style and in its main theme, the richly resonant contrast and fusion of feelings of guilt with the overpowering passion exhaled by some young Greek for a mysterious woman who has bewitched him (she is perhaps a priestess). The interplay and fusion are strongest in the sestet ('noirs enchantements', 'sinistres charmes'), emphasized by the triply alternating rhymes (only one other sonnet in *Les Trophées*—'Epigramme funéraire', p. 50—has a similarly rhymed sestet).

5–6 refer to the hereditary function of the descendants of Eumolpos, priests of Demeter in Eleusis (Heredia changes the place to Samothrace): they judged crimes of impiety, pronouncing imprecations against the delinquent and shaking their cloaks (purple by tradition, 'sanglants' in

Heredia) 'vers le seuil', viz. the house of the person accursed, who was then pursued by the Furies (l. 8, 'les chiens sacrés').

Sphinx

Unpublished before *Les Trophées*, 1893

The sphinx was a fabulous creature with the head, neck and breasts of a woman, the body and claws of a lion and eagle's wings. Confined to Mount Citheron, it pillaged the countryside, devouring those inhabitants who could not decipher its enigmas. It was attributed with a lascivious character: it imparted both terror and sensual pleasure. The sphinx provided a popular theme for poets of the nineteenth century (e.g. Jean Richepin's 'Le Baiser de la Chimère' and Albert Samain's 'Chimère') but Heredia's sonnet drew its inspiration from a sculpture by Ernest Christophe entitled *Le Suprême Baiser*, which he had seen in the musée du Luxembourg. Christophe's sphinx, with the feet and legs of a chimera, receives the kiss of the man who has dared to approach her, while fastening her nails in his breast. On the sculpture's pedestal could be read the following lines by Leconte de Lisle:

> Heureux qui, possédant la Chimère éternelle,
>
> Livre au monstre divin un cœur ensanglanté,
>
> Et savoure, pour mieux s'anéantir en elle,
>
> L'extase de la mort et de la volupté,
>
> Dans l'éclair d'un baiser qui vaut l'éternité!

Like the sculpture, Heredia's hero Bellepheron symbolizes man's sacrifice of self to the consuming illusion of the ideal. The sonnet is built on the quick, antiphonal dialogue between man and sphinx, which contrasts his bravery with her death-dealing sensuality and rises in tone to the final rather facile climax of his death, another typical, if only implicit, oxymoron in its fusion of pain and delight. No other sonnet in *Les Trophées* contains such quick, compact dialogue.

Marsyas

La Revue libre, no. 117, May 1888

The mythical satyr Marsyas (cf. l. 14) is linked with the origins of Greek music. He defied with his primitive flute the divine lyre of Apollo. For this irreverence, Marsyas was beaten and skinned alive. Heredia's sonnet, based on three epigrams from the Greek Anthology, is a tender elegiac lament on Marsyas's fate. The ending is scarcely climactic; it fades away on the perspective of the satyr's skin blowing in the wind. Ibrovac sees the poem as Heredia's defence of all unrecognized artists, a monument to those who have been martyred for their devotion to free art.

5. *Le jaloux Citharède*: viz. jealousy inspired in the Greek zither-player who sang to his own accompaniment.

8. *Célène*: Marsyas became the hero of the town where he originated.
13. *Méandre*: the river Meander has its source in Phrygia.

PERSEE ET ANDROMEDE

All three sonnets in *Revue des deux mondes*, 15 May 1885
Andromeda was the daughter of Cepheus, king of Ethiopia, and Cassiopea. The latter was foolish enough to vie with the Nereids or sea-nymphs for the title of the most beautiful in the land. Neptune avenged his nymphs by sending a sea-monster to ravage the country. The oracle, when consulted, said that Cassiopea's daughter must be tied to a rock and exposed there for the monster to do as it pleased. Andromeda was near to death when Perseus, on his winged horse Pegasus, came to her rescue.

Andromède au monstre
The first line establishes the explicit pathos of Andromeda's plight ('Vierge Céphéenne' because she is the daughter of Cepheus) and the rest of the quatrain may seem purely pictorial: black, hard rock, the sobbing, twisting body of the beauty in distress, the shiver to which proud royal flesh is reduced. But the repetition of nasals, of the vowels *é* and *i* and the consonants *r* and *l*, in brief, the range of positions and sounds through which the reader's mouth is led gives life and felt zest to the visual aspect. The second quatrain is much more fierce in its condensed violence, devoted wholly to the fearsome impressions created by the monster. Yet details are also suggestively implied: the cold feet, the eyelashes closed through fear, the countless teeth ('innombrable'). The sounds of l. 6 are especially forceful: for Ibrovac (ii, p. 464) the gutturals and sibilants alternating with labials or lip consonants suggest the sound of the waves crashing on the rocks. In a manner now familiar, the octet becomes a background against which the sestet can develop its effects: first the thunderbolt suddenness of Pegasus's neighing, then the sudden climax of Andromeda's reaction to this (typically, a fusion of opposites: horror and ecstacy); then the further, more slowly mounting climax as the shadow of the prancing Pegasus heralds the triumphantly heroic arrival of its master. Worth particular note is the emphatic, almost bounding rhythm of the second hemistich in l. 13 (stresses on *fi'ls*, *Ʒe'us*, *Péga'se*), leading with *enjambement* into l. 14 which, by its more conventional rhythm, its nasals and its meaning, connotes extension, relaxation and resolution of difficulty.

Persée et Andromède
The effects here are similar to those of the previous sonnet. The monster's defeat and its horrible appearance are briefly recalled. As before, the

vigorous, prancing liveliness of Pegasus animates the scene. The climax of Pegasus's take-off comes fairly brusquely. Andromeda is contrasted twice with the winged horse, in the second quatrain (its vigour with her sobbing gratitude) and, more forcefully, when woman and horse are each given a tercet (her feebleness is contrasted with Pegasus's zooming strength). We note the artist's eye seeking pictorial and elegantly aesthetic effect in these contrasts and in the (too?) prettily picturesque detail of l. 11.

2 and 5. Chrysaor and Pegasus were both born from the blood of the Medusa when the Gorgon's head was cut off by Perseus. *Chrysaor* means: 'carrying a sword of gold' (he was so born).

Le Ravissement d'Andromède

Heredia evokes the final destiny of Perseus and Andromeda: they were transformed into constellations by Jupiter. This sonnet is certainly competent, but it is perhaps the weakest of the triptych. It seems more obviously written for its dazzlingly starry climax, which too powerfully overshadows the quatrains (the second quatrain is the weaker, in its attempt to convey distance covered). Clichés are made to seem more obvious than usual ('nuit bleue', 'éther étoilé', 'tiède berceau') and there is the unfortunate repetition in 'étoilé' (l. 4), 'd'étoiles en étoiles' (l. 10).

8. Hellas and her brother were fleeing from their father and stepmother on the golden-fleeced ram provided by Jupiter when, over the Bosporus, Hellas fell off (hence the name *Hellespont*, 'the sea of Hellas').

13. The 'Bélier' (Aries or the Ram) and the 'Verseau' (Aquarius or the Water-bearer) are constellations.

EPIGRAMMES ET BUCOLIQUES

See the Introduction, p. 10.

Le Chevrier

Revue des deux mondes, 1 January 1888

Mount Maenalus (l. 3), in Arcadia, was consecrated to Pan, who is introduced in the first tercet. He was the god of shepherds and goatherds and the Greeks associated him with the higher hills where summer pastures were to be found; on moonlit nights, his pipe-playing guided the fauns'—and here, the goats'—dancing. Hecate (l. 8) was worshipped as a goddess of heaven (as Phoebe or the moon) and also as an underworld divinity of spells and witchcraft. The animation of this sonnet's direct apostrophe (shown too by 'Les Bergers') is augmented by the anticipation of Pan's arrival and his actual appearance in the second tercet. But the climax and general tone are fairly muted by comparison with many of the sonnets preceding this subsection. Both 'Le Chevrier'

and 'Les Bergers' have something of the easy familiarity of relaxed con-
versation, though the interlocutor never in fact speaks.

Les Bergers
Revue des deux mondes, 1 January 1888
This sonnet forms a diptych with 'Le Chevrier'. On Mount Cyllene, in
Arcadia, shepherds bring a sheep as tribute to Pan (the 'il' of l. 2). The
pine beneath which Pan is pictured as piping and sleeping derives its
name from the nymph Pitys, who was loved by Pan and turned into a
pine-tree when fleeing from him. As in 'Le Chevrier', Heredia contrasts
the quiet octet with the more dramatic sestet where Pan appears or
nearly appears. The shepherds depart out of awe of Pan and because the
sun is setting in climactic radiance. The last two lines form a resonantly
serene *pointe*, a *trait de morale* which has a kind of evangelical force trans-
cending the context: the lines crystallize the purity and gentle peaceful-
ness present in this and the previous sonnet.

Epigramme votive
Revue des deux mondes, 1 January 1888
The old warrior is about to retire and hang up his weapons. Happy to
accept his lot, he is proud of the bravery he has shown in past exploits.
Thauziès and Zilliacus (see Bibliography) showed that this sonnet owes
something to several epigrams in the Greek Anthology. The dramatic
devices are effective, if obvious and familiar: direct and vigorous
apostrophe, invocation, poignant contrast between past strength and
present feebleness, the dwelling in the tercets on the detail of the empty
quiver which leads to the climactic image of arrows buried in the enemy's
throat.

  1. *Arès*: one of the gods on Olympus who presided over wars. *Dis-
corde*: another Greek god who loved to provoke quarrels and dissensions.
  13. *Marathon*: the famous battle of 490 B.C. when the Greeks under
Miltiades defeated the Persians.

Epigramme funéraire
Revue des deux mondes, 1 January 1888
Being another epigram, the sonnet forms an explicit diptych with the
previous one.
  The epigrammatic quality here derives from the elegiac lament over
the death of the smallest of creatures, a grasshopper. If the sonnet now
seems too fragilely affected and the tercets' images forced and precious,
Heredia draws his inspiration from another age when, as revealed by
recurring images in several epigrams of the Greek Anthology, the sound
of the insect's feet rubbing against each other or against its wings was
seen as Nature's lyre.

Grammont (p. 251) draws attention to the repetition of light vowels in the octet, which serve to 'peindre à l'oreille tout objet ténu, petit, léger, mignon'.

2. *La jeune Hellé*: see commentary for 'Le Ravissement d'Andromède'. 'Epigramme funéraire' and 'La Magicienne' are the only sonnets in *Les Trophées* where the tercets rhyme CDCDCD, in the 'Italian' style used by Ronsard.

Le Naufragé
La Revue blanche, 25 January 1893

This funeral epigram may serve as a typical example of the patchwork of influences that can be discerned in Heredia's work. The Greek Anthology, of course, is the main source. Thauziès showed that the first quatrain owed much to an epigram by the Theban poet Perses, epigram no. 539: 'Sans te préoccuper du funeste coucher de l'Arcture pluvieux, tu t'es embarqué, Théotime, et ton navire bien équipé t'a conduit . . . à travers la mer Egée jusque chez Pluton'. Zilliacus noted 'le Lever de l'Arcture' (Arcturus, double star of the constellation Auriga, the Waggoner) in epigram no. 392 and, for the second tercet, the end of epigram no. 628: 'O terre amoncelée sur cette tombe, ô mer qui baignes ce rivage, soyez pour l'enfant l'une légère, l'autre silencieuse'. Théophile Gautier has 'flancs doublés de cuivre' in 'Portail' (*La Comédie de la mort*, 1838).

The strongest contrast in the sonnet is between the speedy, exhilarating departure in the first quatrain and the mournful end depicted in the second. ' "Le Naufragé" est un *Requiem*' says Ibrovac (ii, p. 443); the sonnet's climax is appropriately quiet, tender and elegiac.

La Prière du mort
Revue des deux mondes, 15 May 1890

This sonnet forms a diptych with 'Le Naufragé'. Cypselo (l. 2) is an ancient city in Spain near the river Ebro. The direct apostrophe gives the sonnet its structure: first, a plea from the spirit of Hyllos's dead son to a passing traveller, begging him to carry news of his death to his father; then, dramatically terse references in the second quatrain to the fate of his corpse and his disconsolate, unavenged ghost; the sestet, briefly recapitulating the octet's sense, begins with a more urgent exhortation to depart and then, with the tender twilight portrayal of his mourning mother at home, the tone undergoes a melodious modification climaxed by the last line's resonant harmonies (of ideas—embrace and tears, love and death, fullness of heart and emptiness of the 'vain tombeau' since his body is not there: of sound—repeated *us*, *is* and *rs*). One is reminded of the beautiful ending of Vigny's 'La Maison du berger':

> Pleurant, comme Diane au bord de ses fontaines,
> Ton amour taciturne et toujours menacé.

7. Erebus is the region above Hell where the souls of the just went to be purified before entering the Elysian Fields. The strong internal rhyme of 'Erèbe enténèbre' is a good instance of Heredia's fondness for intensity and compactness in sounds as well as images. Hyllos's son has been murdered by brigands. Vianey (see Bibliography) reproached Heredia for giving the departed spirit a desire for vengeance alien to the Greek Anthology's epigrams. Ibrovac comments (*Sources*, p. 48): 'ce trait a été ajouté par le poète en souvenir de quelque héros barbare de son maître Leconte de Lisle'.

L'Esclave
La Nouvelle Revue, 15 February 1893

Heredia's love of contrast is shown immediately in the first quatrain—even when treating such a relatively 'tender' subject. The contrast, of state and time, is pointed by the structure of the slave's apostrophe to the 'cher hôte' (someone who has given him refreshment, an innkeeper?): 'tel', such as he describes himself in the first two lines, with all the visible signs of wretched slavery his body bears set against the third and fourth lines, which recall his former proud birthright of happy freedom in Sicily. The pathos implicit in the broken *coupes* of the first two lines contrasts with the sweeping vista and harmony in the picture of Mount Hybla in Sicily, sweet with its honey and sweet to the memory, given felt form by the ample regularity of the rhythms in ll. 3 and 4 as well as by the prevalence of gentle consonants, especially *l*s and *m*s. The evocation of Sicily is felt but also visual, conveying artistic satisfaction in harmonious curves and the convergence of distant objects, mountain tops, in soothing waters. The second quatrain amplifies the nostalgia: thus the implied pathos in the picture of the swans which can return, and choose to return, to Sicily every spring whereas he cannot. How often he must have watched them longingly in their flight! The variations in the *coupes* (6/2/4: 4/5/3: 4/8: 2/4/6), the strong *contre-rejet* between ll. 5 and 6 and the *enjambement* between ll. 6 and 7 help to impart the keenness and swiftness of his longing in a quickly moving clause, from 'si jamais' to 'Tu retournes'. The octet ends with a new element of pathos which will take up all the sestet: the longing for news of his beloved in Sicily. The first tercet embodies his bitter-sweet memory of her, implying that he will probably never see her again: her beauty and purity were one with the Sicily he has evoked. The second tercet, which breaks the memory and returns to the present with a direct appeal for pity, verges on the prosaic in its simplicity (of a kind Verlaine exploited). The last line, in its quiet and plain affirmation of his moving faith in the constancy of his beloved, could scarcely be more different from the type of *vers définitif* traditionally associated with Heredia.

11. However beautiful the image here—its harmony and symmetry

echoing those of ll. 3 and 4—it may seem too sophisticated and precious for the slave to utter and for the simplicity achieved by most of the sonnet. F. Brodel praises the first tercet but asks: 'Pourquoi le dernier vers vient-il en gâter l'harmonie par le luxe d'une métaphore dispropor-tionnée à l'importance du détail qu'elle souligne?' He is critical of the violent, too self-consciously grandiose images and sounds in many sonnets, but observes cogently of 'Le Naufragé', 'La Prière du mort' and 'L'Esclave':

> Avec quel art, cependant, dans ces trois pièces, Heredia termine une période par le dernier vers du premier tercet, avant d'entamer le tercet final auquel il laisse toute la force d'un rappel et d'une con-clusion, mais aussi la douceur, sans rien de théâtral, ni de déclama-toire, de la plainte exténuée qui vient mourir sur les lèvres. (Op. cit., pp. 123–4)

12. The name *Cléariste* is doubtless taken from Leconte de Lisle's poem 'Kléarista' (*Poèmes antiques*, 1852) whose second line is: 'Avec ses noirs sourcils arqués sur ses yeux bleus'.

Le Laboureur

Revue des deux mondes, 15 May 1890

Parmis the ploughman, at the end of his working days, consecrates his tools to Rhea (l. 6), or Cybeles, goddess of the earth and animals. Heredia conveys the dull, patient toil and simple dignity of the plough-man's hard life, concisely summed up in l. 11, with its Cornelian ring. For suggestive contrast and climax in the second tercet, Parmis is shown having difficulty imagining that there really can be true rest for him after death.

14. *Erèbe*: see notes for 'La Prière du mort'.

A Hermès Criophore

La Revue blanche, 25 January 1893

Hermes Criophorus (*Criophorus* derives from two Greek words meaning 'producing sheep or mutton') is 'le compagnon des Naïades' or water-nymphs in l. 1. He was a god of fecundity to whom, as in this sonnet, goats were sacrificed on his altar. He was an important celestial god: *lares* received only incense or fruit.

4. *berges du Galèse*: a river in Calabria near the city of Tarento. The region, in the south-west of Italy, was well-known for its breeding of sheep, cattle and horses.

7. The 'Démon familier' is, of course, Hermes Criophorus. This votive sonnet, 'Le Chevrier' and 'Les Bergers' form a gracious triptych depicting the rural life and beliefs of ancient Greece.

La Jeune Morte

La Lecture, 25 September 1892

The spirit of another corpse addresses a passer-by. Our interest is stimulated and sustained not just by the apostrophe but by the sonnet's cleverly varied rhythms. In l. 4, the vivid juxtaposition of human consciousness with growing ivy and crawling ant is worthy of the early Gautier, but the octet's main emphasis is on the young maiden's solitariness and her poignant regard for the humblest form of the life of which she is now deprived (beautifully captured in the movingly simple inflections of l. 8's direct plea). The first tercet enlarges the pathos of her death with the kind of resolution of opposites we have frequently noted as oxymoron: 'épouse et vierge', 'si proche et déjà loin'. In the second tercet, the cruelty of her eternal exile from light and life is communicated by a wave of expanding suggestion climaxed by the sombre nasals and dark infinity of 'Nuit Ténébreuse' and 'inexorable Erèbe' (see commentary for 'La Prière du mort').

Regilla

Revue des deux mondes, 1 February 1893

By its theme, this sonnet forms a diptych with 'La Jeune Morte'. It is closely modelled on an epitaph in the Greek Anthology to the memory of Annia Regilla, adored wife of Herod the Athenian (l. 3): he built an exedra (l. 1, 'ce marbre') in her honour. Ibrovac (*Sources*, p. 53) quotes the relevant part of the epitaph:

> Passant, offre-lui un sacrifice . . . Regilla était de l'opulente race des Enéades, du sang illustre d'Anchise et de Vénus Idéenne . . . une des plus charmantes petites-filles d'Enée, une sœur de Ganymède . . . En Grèce nul n'égale en noblesse, n'égale en éloquence, Hérode . . . Pour elle, elle habite parmi les héroïnes dans les îles fortunées où règne Saturne . . . Les noires Parques ont ravi de sa noble demeure la moitié de ses enfants . . . Son auguste et charmante image . . . C'est ainsi que Jupiter a consolé un mari en deuil . . . l'époux au désespoir . . . vieillard désolé qui pleure sur sa couche solitaire. Car Regilla n'est plus une mortelle . . . Son âme s'est abritée sous le sceptre de Rhadamanthe.

2. Her brother Ganymedes, later cup-bearer of the gods. Aphrodite (the Roman Venus) was the mother of the famous Trojan prince Aeneas (l. 3) from whom Regilla is descended.

6. *l'Ile Fortunée*: the Fortunate Isles (now the Canaries) where the Ancients situated their heaven, the Elysian Fields. Their ruler was Saturn, 'le prince infernal' of l. 6.

8. *la Parque*: Atropos. There were three sister divinities called Parcae. Clotho held the distaff, Lachesis spun the thread of life, Atropos cut the thread.

14. *Rhadamante*: judge of the underworld.

In this sonnet, as in 'L'Esclave' and 'La Jeune Morte', Heredia is drawn to express the pain that love can bring, well conveyed by the throbbingly and melodiously insistent nasals of ll. 9 and 10.

Le Coureur
Revue des deux mondes, 15 May 1890

The sonnet follows very closely an anonymous epigram in the Greek Anthology, no. 54, which describes Myron's statue of the runner Ladas, famous in the time of Alexander the Great:

Tel que tu étais lorsque Thymus te suivait léger comme le vent, lorsque, penché en avant, tu effleurais le sol de tes pieds; tel, ô Ladas vivant encore, Myron t'a coulé en bronze, en imprimant sur tout ton corps l'attente de la couronne olympique. Le cœur palpite d'espérance; sur les lèvres on voit le souffle intérieur de la poitrine haletante. Peut-être [bientôt] le bronze va s'élancer vers la couronne, la base même ne le retiendra pas. Le vent est bien rapide, l'art l'est davantage. (Ibrovac, *Sources*, p. 54)

The statue is animated by stressing the panting ribs, the straining muscles and the eager impetus embodied in the statue. The reconciliation or resolution of antitheses (here, panting life and still bronze) is a constant aim for Heredia, as it often was for Gautier. One inevitably recalls the latter's poem 'L'Art' (1858 edition of *Emaux et camées*):

Sculpte, lime, cisèle;
Que ton rêve flottant
Se scelle
Dans le bloc résistant!

Le Cocher
La Revue blanche, 25 January 1893

This descriptive epigram forms a diptych with 'Le Coureur', to which it is similar by its stress on competitive games and success. It is modelled on some twenty-five epigrams in the Greek Anthology devoted to Porphyrus, the Libyan charioteer (l. 8). These epigrams belong to a group of inscriptions found on the socle of the statues of the athletes in the hippodrome at Constantinople. One of these, close to which is another, of Victory (cf. the second tercet), is of Porphyrus, who was much prized by the Emperor Justinian (the 'Autocrator' in l. 8, viz. the absolute power). Porphyrus goes so fast in his chariot that Victory is pictured as flying to greet him.

Sur l'Othrys
Le Temps, 8 September 1889

The Othrys is a chain of mountains in Thessaly (cf. l. 8). The herdsman or shepherd invites his (unexpected?) guest to take his ease and enjoy the beautiful sunset and the glories of the mountain scene visible from his cabin (for his details, by his own admission, Heredia was indebted to a page of *La Grèce d'aujourd'hui* by G. Deschamps: see Ibrovac, *Sources*, p. 56).

7. Olympus and Tymphrestes are mountains.

9. *l'Eubée*: island of the Greek archipelago.

10. *Le Callidrome*: one of Œta's peaks. It was there that Hercules burned himself to death on a pyre built by himself, to end the torment produced by the famous shirt Nessus gave to Hercules's wife and which she gave to her husband. Henceforth, Hercules was worshipped as a god and, in consequence, there had his first altar.

13–14. *Pégase*: see commentary for 'Persée et Andromède'. *Parnasse*: another famous mountain. The tercet's climactic force speaks for itself: Pegasus's name is dramatically held back and in the intervening suspense he thereby creates, between 'Parnasse' and 'Pégase', Heredia condenses the antithetical arrival and departure of the winged horse.

With this sonnet, the section 'La Grèce et la Sicile' closes, as it opened in 'L'Oubli', with a panoramic view of the Grecian landscape.

ROME ET LES BARBARES

See the Introduction, p. 12.

Pour le Vaisseau de Virgile
Revue des deux mondes, 1 January 1888

The cycle of Roman poems opens with an evocation of Virgil's journey to Greece, thus linking these sonnets with the Grecian cycle just completed. The influence of Greece was great on Virgil as on Heredia himself. Much in this sonnet is owed to Horace (*Carmina*, Liber I, iii). The 'dioscures brillants' (l. 2, from two Greek words meaning 'divine children', 'children of Jupiter'), are Castor and Pollux, sons of Jupiter and Leda and brothers of Helen and Clytemnestra: Castor and Pollux were made into the constellation Gemini and became tutelar gods of hospitality, favourable, when both were visible, to navigators. Their blessing is thus appropriately invited for the journey of Virgil, 'le poète latin', to the golden 'Cyclades' (a group of twenty-five islands of the Greek archipelago). Heredia then invokes the assistance of Iapix, the gentlest of the zephyrs or west winds, to speed Virgil's journey to Greece (l. 8, 'rivage étranger'). The gentleness and happiness of the sonnet's mood are reinforced by the reference to the dolphins in l. 9 (cf. the force of 'heureusement' and 'fraternel') and to Arion in l. 13. Arion was a famous Greek poet (circa 620 D.C.) who, according to legend, was thrown into the sea by pirates but was then saved from drowning by dolphins which had been delighted by his playing of the lyre.

10. *le chanteur de Mantoue*: Virgil was born in Mantua, Italy, in 70 B.C.

11. *fils du Cygne*: another reference to Castor and Pollux. Their father, Jupiter, took the form of a swan when he paid court to their mother, Leda.

This sonnet is not gripping in the manner of many of 'La Grèce et la Sicile'. It is meant to acknowledge Heredia's love and respect for Virgil and Greek culture. It also suggests to some extent the characteristic tone and note of the Latin poet, his delicacy, gentleness and harmonious style. There is no surprise (thus, in the second quatrain, clichés abound: 'pousse', 'rivage étranger', 'redoublant son haleine', 'brise embaumée', with a preponderance of gentle consonants).

Villula
Revue des deux mondes, 15 May 1890

Heredia celebrates the wisdom of Gallus who, like the two protagonists of 'Le Laboureur' and 'Le Dieu Hêtre', accepts his 'destin borné' (l. 12) and finds contentment in the simple life and possessions whose details make up the poem. Some sentences (e.g. ll. 5, 8, 12–14) have a Latin concision.

2. *cisalpin*: on the Roman side of the Alps.

6. *plus d'un pain* is weak padding.

La Flûte
Revue des deux mondes, 15 May 1890

Heredia reanimates a commonplace of bucolic poetry: the speaker encourages some goatherd to soothe his state of fevered love by playing his pipes in the gentle evening peace of his rural setting. The 'Qu'accompagne' in l. 4 is found cacophonous by most readers: a rare fault in Heredia. With regard to the first tercet, Ibrovac (ii, p. 458) writes of 'ces rejets assez faibles': perhaps, but not by the liberated standards of Verlaine and Mallarmé who, like Heredia here, often fused lines together into one lyrical sentence of varied inflections.

12. Silenus was a Trojan god, father of the satyrs and foster-father of Bacchus. He was skilled in pipe-playing.

A Sextius
La Vie moderne, 25 March 1882

This is a very close adaptation of Horace's famous ode (*Carmina*, Liber I, viii), dedicated to the consul Sestius, who was appointed in 23 B.C. Like Horace, Heredia describes spring and the shortness of life; he invites us to enjoy what pleasure we can. The melancholy is stronger in Heredia than in Horace. Heredia enlivens an eternal commonplace of poetry by the strong contrast between the first and second quatrains, between the themes of death and spring or the hedonistic enjoyment of life. The tones vary with the length of the sentences, concise, clipped, even harsh (first tercet) or more suggestively long, implying tranquil pleasure (second tercet) or sombre bitterness concerning remembered delights that will cease.

7–8. The *symposiarch* or king of the feast was usually chosen by throwing dice. It was his duty to determine the dosage of water in the wine (the Greeks did not drink pure wine). He also settled in advance the number of drinks for each person.

13. Faunus was a Roman rural god, protector of flocks and herds.

HORTORUM DEUS

See the Introduction, p. 13.

I

La Revue indépendante, March 1888

The dedication is to Paul Arène, anonymous author—with several others equally anonymous—of *Le Parnassiculet contemporain, recueil de vers nouveaux*, December 1866, a collection intended as pastiches and parodies of the poems that had begun to appear, from March of that year, in *Le Parnasse contemporain*. Heredia contributed to the latter and was gently mocked in the former. Another contributor to *Le Parnasse contemporain*, Catulle Mendès, did not like the way he had been treated and came near to provoking a duel with Paul Arène. Heredia clearly took himself less seriously, in public at least: one assumes he thought the comic tone of 'Hortorum Deus' would please Arène.

The epigraph from Horace (*Carmina*, Liber I, viii):

> Olim truncus eram ficulnus, inutile lignum,
> Cum faber, incertus scamnum faceretne Priapum,
> Maluit esse Deum

can be translated: 'I was a useless fig-tree when the workman, uncertain whether to make a bench or a Priapus from my trunk, chose the second'.

Fiercely, and with an element of exaggeration partly comic in his very eloquence, the god Priapus warns off a potential intruder into the garden he is protecting. He summons all the dignity he can: however abject and laughable he may now appear (l. 7), he is still a god of noble origin and threatens to use his powers. The abusive and vigorous apostrophe in the octet leads, in the sestet, to a sadly nostalgic and lyrical contrast between his former joyous roaming over the seas as a ship's prow and his present lowly lot. The robust familiarity of tone in the octet strongly distinguishes this sonnet from the decorous restraint of many in *Les Trophées*.

6. *Egine*: an island in the Greek archipelago. It had a variety of woods, including the poorly regarded fig-tree, used to make busts and

statues of Priapus and other minor gods. The wood was so little prized
that the Greeks used the pejorative phrase *man of fig*. It had much sap:
since Priapus was a god of generation, he was appropriately cut from the
most fertile tree. 'Egine' may be an allusion to a school of Greek archi-
tecture.

2. *j'imagine* is padding and there for the rhyme.

14. *Cyclades*: see the commentary for 'Pour le vaisseau de Virgile'.

II

With *III, IV* and *V*, in *Le Mercure de France*, February 1892.

The epigraph from Catullus, *Carmina*, XIX and XX (meaning: 'For its
masters worship me and hail me as a god'), again indicates the source.

Priapus enjoys the simple life of the orchard garden: in return for his
protection, the humble peasants bedeck him and twice a year sacrifice a
young goat in his honour.

As Grammont notes (p. 75), the trimeter in l. 2 is clumsy.

III

The epigraph ('Here comes the farmer') is from Catullus's *Carmen*, XX
which, with XIX, again provides most of Heredia's details. Priapus is
watching over his garden; his speech is ejaculatory and familiar as he
apostrophizes the children about to steal the fruit. The snares and traps
are daunting enough; the mention of the dog is even more sudden and
startling (given the *enjambement*, throwing emphasis onto the two syllables
of 'Au chien!'). Priapus knows what children are like (using the pretext
of coming for a clump of garlic to steal fruit and grapes). In the very
aggressiveness of his tone there is implicit a certain indulgent under-
standing of children's ways. The repetitive sound of 'grappiller ma
grappe' must be intentionally comic. The second quatrain goes further
in this direction with the emphatic *coupes* of l. 6 (6/1/2/3) and its comic
imprecation ('par mon pieu!') and the inherently comic device of using
the rhetorical eloquence of ll. 7–8 to describe something as prosaic as a
wallop. We would usually think in this context of a man using a piece of
wood to spank a naughty child; here, the roles are amusingly reversed,
man becomes the tool and the wood the agent. The god Priapus is
assuming a mock self-importance. The short syllables ('bras d'homme
qui frappe') strengthen the idea of violent thumps. In the sestet, Priapus
is indulgently aiding and abetting the children, telling them how to get
to a neighbouring orchard where stealing will be easy: the strong *en-
jambement* in the first tercet helps to create the direct familiarity of con-
versational address. The last two lines change the tone: the ending is
pictorial, suggesting the sensuous delight of vines and the cool ease of
their shade.

IV

Catullus is again closely followed: the epigraph ('In spring, a brightly coloured garland is put on me') is from his *Carmen*, XX. Priapus conveys his peaceful happiness in receiving the offerings brought by each season of the year. Life is again depicted as simple, upright and humble, for him as for the family whose property he protects. The image in the last two lines is visual and auditory: Grammont argues (pp. 248–9) that the light vowels (*fait, tinter, main, deniers, clair*) 'sont aptes à exprimer un bruit ténu, clair'. But sounds are not separable from ideas: the conclusive couplet expresses the uncomplicated and untroubled pleasure found by humble folk in money honestly earned.

V

The epigraph ('My beard is tough and stiff with ice') is from the *Priapeia*, a collection of epigrams attributed to Ovid, Catullus, Tibullus, Martial and other Latin poets and all relating to Priapus (Ibrovac, *Sources*, p. 69). Abandoned, dilapidated and freezing as he awaits the warmth of sunrise, the scarecrow Priapus laments the hard lot of a rustic god. In the tercets, with a loquacity partly sad and partly tinged with a bitterly comic note (cf. the repetition in 'repeint, repu'), he envies the comfortable life of the *penates* and *lares*, domestic gods of the Romans who were represented by small statues in people's homes and fêted with honey, fruit and flowers. He would then have had a warm and respected place.

3. *Soracte*: a mountain. This is a reminiscence of Horace (*Carmina*, I, 9).

7. *vermillon*: Priapus's statues were painted red to discourage birds, animals and intruders.

13–14. The 'jour viril' was 17 March, the date of Bacchus's festival. It was then, at the age of seventeen, that the young Roman put aside the *bulla* or locket he had carried from birth as a charm, hanging it on the neck of the domestic *lar* (l. 14). In exchange, his father would give him a white toga, marking the adolescent's entry into society and adult life.

Le Tepidarium
Le Siècle littéraire, 18 November 1875

This sonnet may serve as another good instance of the patchwork of influences that can be detected in much of Heredia's work. His first and main inspiration was Chassériau's painting (in the Louvre) which has the same title as the sonnet. Painting and poem reveal the same scene of the steam-bath and the same reflections of the brazier on pale faces (ll. 3–4); Heredia's octet provides a background for the 'femme d'Asie' who corresponds in position, gesture and effect to the standing woman in Chassériau's painting, set against the background of the women seated in the steam-bath. Painting and poem exude a similar atmosphere of sophisticatedly voluptuous *décadence*, that is, not just the decadence of Rome but what is implied in literary terms by the word *décadence* in the nineteenth century (cf. the conclusion in ll. 13–14). The sonnet, like the painting, is animated by the interplay of light and shadow (cf. l. 14): both exploit the plastic sense of shapes and outlines.

But pictorial models or visual inspirations are not separable for Heredia from verbal and literary reminiscences. Ibrovac suggests possible literary sources in lines of Gautier, Leconte de Lisle, Glatigny and Banville (*Sources*, pp. 71–2). Thauziès showed that l. 1 is composed of two hemistiches from two lines of different poems by Leconte de Lisle:

> *La myrrhe a parfumé* leurs barbes vénérables
> > 'La Vigne de Naboth' (*Poèmes barbares*)
> L'huile baigne à doux flots *leurs membres assouplis*
> > 'Niobé' (*Poèmes antiques*)

It is very unlikely that this is conscious plagiarism: the phrases must have been deeply embedded in Heredia's memory.

The sound effects in this sonnet would repay a particularly close study. Thus, in ll. 3–4, the languor of the sense is partly created by the interplay of nasals (especially 'bronze', 'chambre', 'ombre', occurring at key points, sixth or twelfth syllables of the line) and consonants (especially *b*s and *l*s).

11. Provides an interesting fusion of opposites, restless movement ('tord') and bored repose ('ennui serein'). Such resolutions of contrasts are favourite devices in Heredia, as we have seen when noting oxymoron. The line achieves an effect of arrested movement, partly comparable with that of the words italicised in Baudelaire's evocation in his poem 'L'Idéal':

> Ou bien toi, grande Nuit, fille de Michel-Ange,
> Qui *tords paisiblement* dans une pose étrange
> Tes appas façonnés aux bouches des Titans!

12. *Ausonie*: town in Italy. Poets often use *Ausonia* to mean all Italy.

Tranquillus
La Nouvelle Revue, 15 February 1893

Caius Suetonius Tranquillus was a famous Latin historian, grammarian and rhetorician, born about 70 B.C., secretary to the Emperor Hadrian. In the letter of Pliny the Younger referred to in the epigraph, Heredia noted that Suetonius, at the time Pliny was writing, was preparing to buy a modest country-house (l. 2) some 30 kms. from Rome, near to the city of Tibur (l. 2, now Tivoli). Tivoli was famous for its enchanting sites, celebrated by Horace, and its country seats. Heredia's sonnet is, typically, built on a contrast: amid the peace of this rural setting, Suetonius recorded on his tablets (ll. 12–13) the turbulence and violence of imperial circles in Rome. Ll. 9–10 recall infamous figures: the Emperor Nero (Lucius Domicius), who was adopted by the Emperor Claudius when the latter married Agrippina the Younger, Nero's mother. Messalina was the previous wife of the Emperor Claudius: she horrified society with her crimes. The Emperor Caligula was the son of Agrippina the Elder and Germanicus: his madness and cruelty are legendary.

14. The old man is the Emperor Tiberius who retired to the imperial palace on the island of Capri where he was alleged to have surrendered to dreadful excesses ('noirs loisirs').

Only one other sonnet in *Les Trophées* ('La Vision de Khèm II') has a similar rhyme-scheme in the tercets: CCDDCD.

Lupercus

Unpublished before *Les Trophées*, 1893

This sonnet is almost a translation of the epigram by Martial referred to in the epigraph (Ibrovac, *Sources*, p. 72). Lupercus, a mediocre scribbler, wants to read Martial's latest work by borrowing rather than buying it. Martial declines and indicates where it can be had, from the book-seller Atrectus in the Argiletum (l. 8), a Roman suburb which contained various bookshops and artisans' shops.

9. The Forum, situated between the Capitol and the Palatine Hill (l. 7) was where assemblies debated public affairs.

11. All five were, of course, Roman authors.

12. By a poetic convention, the *s* of *certes* is dropped so that the line contains just twelve syllables.

The last line's climax is sardonically deflating.

La Trebbia

Revue des deux mondes, 15 May 1890

Heredia owes many of his details to Livy (Liber XXI, ch. 52–7, Liber XXII, ch. 54–6). The Roman consul Sempronius had defeated Hannon, one of the best lieutenants of the Carthaginian leader, Hannibal, in a battle in Spain (hence l. 7). With Publius Cornelius Scipio, who had already been defeated by Hannibal at Tesino, he attacked Hannibal's forces on the banks of the river Trebbia, in Italy, in 218 B.C. The Romans could not resist the fierce and fast Numidian (i.e. Algerian) horsemen (l. 3). Both consuls fell, and 30,000 Romans with them. It is the scene before the defeat which Heredia describes with forceful economy: the sinister dawn seeming to herald doom, the exotic detail of the trumpeters vibrantly arousing the camp, the signs and weather conditions that should have discouraged the Romans from attacking Hannibal, the ravaged and burning villages. The first eleven lines are a background and preparation for the brilliantly contrasting climax in the second tercet: with a dramatic switch, Heredia singles out the genius Hannibal who, in contrast with the plodding Sempronius and the moving Romans, is casually leaning against a bridge's arch, still, thoughtful and triumphant as he listens to the dull trampling of the marching legions. With a wave of suggestion, the perspective is widened immensely in the last line, which suggests all the as yet unleashed power and expectancy of the battle to come. Hannibal is triumphant because he knows that he has hidden his brother's troops in the marshy grasses and undergrowth between the rival camps; they will attack the Romans in the rear. For us, the elephants (l. 11) are an exotic detail: historically, they were important in the battle. Livy says that their strange appearance and smell frightened the Romans' horses and caused chaos. As Ibrovac points out (ii, p. 367), the trumpeting of the elephants is one detail in a tableau of sound (river, trumpeters, soldiers).

5. *augures*: Roman soothsayers who foretold future events by omens.

8. These are the marks of departure. A Roman consul was attended by twelve lictors, officers carrying axes encircled with *fasces* or sticks.

10. *Insubres*: after the battle of Tesino, these people had united with Hannibal. The Romans therefore burned their villages.

All the sonnet's rhymes are *rares*, save *fleuve-s'abreuve* and *éléphant-triomphant*.

Après Cannes
Revue des deux mondes, 15 May 1890
The battle of Cannae (a small village in Apulia on the banks of the river Aufidus) took place in 216 B.C. The two consuls defeated by Hannibal's forces were Terentius Barron and Paulus Emilius. It was the latter who lay dead on the field of battle, the other fleeing to Venusa (l. 2). The strong *enjambements* in the first quatrain help to convey the disorder and defeat of battle, the suddenness of the thunderbolt. But Heredia dwells mostly on the consternation in Rome, the fear of Hannibal and the sinister omens (related by Livy, Liber XXII, ch. 7) auguring Hannibal's march on the capital (ll. 3–4). To appease the gods, sacrifices were offered and for three days the Romans celebrated a *lectisternium*, a sacrifice which entailed placing the gods on couches or platforms in the temples, before the people (l. 5). The Sibylline books (l. 6), a collection of oracles concerning Rome's destiny, were always consulted in times of calamity. Suburra (l. 11) was a district of Rome noted for its iniquity. The *ergastula* (l. 11) were prisons for slaves. Hannibal's elephant Getulus is the one described by Juvenal (*Saturae* X, l. 158).

'La Trebbia' is set before the battle, 'Après Cannes' comes after a battle: Heredia's emphasis is on the human implications of war, expectancy or consternation. This study in panic acquires its power from the close details. It reaches three small peaks of intensity (l. 4, ll. 7–8, l. 11) but the highest point, towards which the whole poem is tensed, comes in the shape of the anxiously awaited Hannibal, whose sinisterly exotic, one-eyed appearance is anticipated in the waning light of a sympathetically sanguinary sunset (the sun too is depicted as a single eye).

1. *Linterne* is there for the rhyme. There is no historical authority for the reference: Linterna was in the opposite direction from Venusa.

A un Triomphateur
Revue des deux mondes, 15 May 1890
This sonnet forms a triptych with 'La Trebbia' and 'Après Cannes'. Heredia's point of departure is Juvenal's *Saturae*, X, ll. 133–46, where the Latin poet's theme is the twists of fortune undergone by Hannibal and his sad end (l. 133 of Juvenal's satire was given as an epigraph when the sonnet was first published). Several details are borrowed, especially in the first quatrain (Ibrovac, *Sources*, p. 77). Juvenal attacks the thirst for titles engraved in marble, revealing disgust that man is more concerned about fame than virtue. For Juvenal's fundamentally moral preoccupation Heredia substitutes a more or less philosophical one lending itself to a striking picture and lapidary concision. The animating apostrophe is characteristic, this time directly from Heredia to the emperor who symbolizes all famous men: equally characteristic is the contrast between octet and sestet. However much the emperor tries to preserve his name and glories, time through nature will erode them. The second tercet is reminiscent of Virgil's famous 'Scilicet et tempus veniet' (*Georgicon*, Liber I, ll. 493–7). The sonnet's thought, images and language give it some of the hardness and sculpturesque difficulty recommended by Gautier in his poem 'L'Art'.

4. The *rostrum* was the ram of an ancient warship, the *aplustrum* was the ornamental stern.

5. Ancus Martius was the fourth legendary king of Rome.

14. The Samnites (of Samnium, former region of ancient Italy) were one of the warlike tribes who resisted Rome, in the fourth century B.C.

ANTOINE ET CLEOPATRE

All three sonnets in *Le Monde poétique*, 1884
Few subjects have captured the imagination of historians and artists more than that of Mark Anthony and his dalliance with Cleopatra, queen of Egypt. Many models could have influenced Heredia, particularly Plutarch (*Life of Mark Anthony*) and Shakespeare (*Anthony and Cleopatra*): in publications before *Les Trophées*, 'Le Cydnus' had an epigraph from Plutarch while quotations from *Anthony and Cleopatra* formed the epigraphs of the other two sonnets. Other literary sources were Gautier and Banville (see Ibrovac, *Sources*, p. 80). For the most part, Heredia shuns particular historical detail, concentrating on the universal

significance of the two figures, the great warrior who lost all through love, the voluptuous, ambitious queen. Triumph and catastrophe are climactically joined in the first and third of these sonnets.

Le Cydnus

The Cydnus is the river navigated by Cleopatra's galley in all its finery when she was summoned by Mark Anthony to Tarsus (l. 9), a city in Asia Minor. Though their styles are of course very different, Shakespeare's famous description of the barge (*Anthony and Cleopatra*, II. ii, ll. 199–226) shares certain details (e.g. colour and perfume) with Heredia's, through their common debt to Plutarch. With fine economy, the first quatrain sets the scene: blazing heat from blue sky, the interplay of colours on the water (*argent, blanchit, noir*), the voluptuousness of smells and sounds. The sparrow-hawk (l. 5) was the sacred bird of Egypt, the form taken by the immortal soul after death: its head and folded wings form the queen's golden helmet. In Plutarch, Shakespeare, Gautier and Banville, Cleopatra is lying down. Heredia puts her stretched forward at the boat's prow, a plastic and sculpturesque detail, of course, but psychologically cogent as well and prolonging the implications of *épervier*, for it enables Heredia to sum up her rapacious dominance. All Anthony's defection from duty and surrender to love are implied by the 'guerrier désarmé' (l. 9) whom Cleopatra's arms are dramatically open to welcome. In l. 11, Heredia develops further nuances of colour as the setting sun beams on Cleopatra's skin: the line is beautifully incantatory, magic in meaning and sound, owing much to the repeated *r*s and the sensuous nasals at key points (*ambre, pourpre, roses*) and to the range of vowel sounds, heavier in the first hemistich, lighter in colour and sound in the second. In Plutarch, Shakespeare and Banville, Cleopatra is accompanied by young children likened to Cupids. Heredia keeps two attendants for the conclusive contrast of the second tercet. Eros becomes Lust and the other figure is Death, both symbolic of human destiny and of Cleopatra's life and eventual fate.

10. The Lagides were an Egyptian dynasty (306 to 30 B.C.).

Soir de bataille

The Roman soldiers under Mark Anthony have just suffered heavy casualties in a battle with the Parthians. The king of these famous archers was Fraates (l. 7: one of Heredia's manuscripts—Bibliothèque Nationale, Nouv. Acq. 14828 f. 46—gives the name Fraates but he changes the rhymes and then substitutes, for the rhyme, Fraortes, a legendary king of Medea).

The octet has two panels: the first quatrain depicts the efforts of the Roman officers to rally their troops amid the harsh aftermath of battle (with strong use of *r*s and a typical union of contrasting impressions in the savouring of bitter smells, 'âcres parfums', l. 4); the second quatrain is entirely devoted to the dejection and sweating fatigue of the ordinary troops. The sonnet is hinged on l. 9, with its past historic tense strikingly contrasted with the imperfects in the octet. The appearance of Anthony is further dramatized by delaying the subject of the verb *apparut* until the last words of the sonnet; between verb and subject and against the background of discouragement, dull colour and tiredness in the octet, we have one of the most vibrantly compact sestets in *Les Trophées*. Anthony is all warm colour ('rouge', 'vermeil', 'blessures fraîches', 'pourpre', 'rutilant', 'enflammé', 'sanglant'), splendour, mettlesome energy and sonorous hardness (cf. l. 12). The imperial purple denotes his rank as does the flourish of trumpets; his horse may shy but this serves only to set off Anthony's power of command. Even Anthony has suffered wounds, but they help to enhance his courage and strength as, in a typical fusion of horror and ecstasy, he is etched climactically in the last line against a sympathetically flaming sky. The poem's perspectives are important: background ('archers de Phraortes'), middle ground (Roman soldiers), foreground (Anthony). Two rhymes (ll. 1 and 4, 5 and 8) are poor, but the others are hard and resounding, especially in the sestet, in accord with the scene's bellicose grandeur. Another aspect of the language is the unflamboyant authenticity of various *mots justes*. There were six *tribunes* or superior officers to a Roman legion of 6000 soldiers. A legion was composed of ten *cohorts*, a cohort therefore consisting of 600 men. The cohort was further subdivided into six *centurias*, that is, each of 100 men, each under the command of a *centurion*.

Antoine et Cléopâtre

This is probably the most famous of Heredia's sonnets, and deservedly. From the start, the couple dominate the scene ('de la haute terrasse'), standing out as impressive figures and legendary lovers. The scene they observe is the setting for the poem, sultry and oppressive with the evening heat and the thick, heavy Nile: the names Bubasta and Saïs, important town at that time in lower Egypt, provide further local colour and exoticism. The rhythms play their part: the two stronger breaks in ll. 1 and 3 throw greater emphasis on the flowing vistas of ll. 2 and 4. The context set, Heredia moves to a close-up of the lovers' ecstatic embrace and a piquant contrast between the heavy armour of the strong soldier, epitome of conquering virility and martial prowess, and the soft, languorous delight of Cleopatra's body ('ployer', 'défaillir', 'corps voluptueux'). But within this contrast is a further antithesis, in l. 6: Anthony is a slave to Cleopatra and his erotic dream. The subservience of lover to mistress is developed in the sestet: he is swooningly in the power of her aggressive, dominant eroticism, conveyed with the sharp clarity of telling visual images (l. 11—cf. 'Le Cydnus', l. 8). The second tercet continues the erotic stance and the notion of his dependence ('sur elle courbé') before leading into the brilliantly suggestive climax of the last two lines. In her eyes, Anthony sees the reflection of fleeing galleys, a glimpse of the defeat to be inflicted on them by Octavius Caesar and Agrippa in the sea-battle of Actium in 31 B.C. Baudelaire, who ends his sonnet 'Les Chats' with an image of partly comparable nature, position and suggestion, would have delighted in the thematically founded and imaginatively liberating link between the small area of gold-specked irises and the huge vista of sea and ships.

SONNETS EPIGRAPHIQUES

See the Introduction, p. 14.

Le Vœu

Les Lettres et les arts, 1 March 1886

V.S.L.M. are the initials of 'votum solvit libens merito (or liberata malo)'. The epigraphs are two authentic inscriptions, the first meaning: 'To the god Ilixon from Fabia Festa, in just fulfilment of a spontaneous vow', the second, 'To the god Iscitt, from Hunnu, son of Ulohox, etc.'. Fabia Festa is a Roman woman's name found in inscriptions on pillars, statues and columns in the area. The other is a Gallic name.

1–2. The Iberians were the oldest people of Western Europe. They inhabited Spain, southern Gaul and parts of northern Italy. The Galls were the Celts, the Garumni the Gascons.

5. *Venasque*: synecdoche for people from a town in France, four kms. from Carpentras (now in the *département* of Vaucluse).

The historical inspiration gives the poem's antithetic perspective: past (octet), present (sestet).

La Source

La Jeune France, 1 November 1882

The epigraph ('sacred to the venerable nymphs') is again authentic. It was found on a votive altar unearthed in 1762 in a former chapel of the thermal baths at Luchon and due no doubt to some grateful invalid cured by the waters there. Heredia replaces the stone near a sacred spring which it must have indicated. The nymph of the spring who was once offered sacrifices on the altar is now sadly neglected. The octet evokes her solitariness and abandonment; in l. 2, as Grammont remarks (p. 212), all the emphases fall on the vowels *ou* or *om*—*source, nom, goutte, tombe*—which are musically interlinked. See Ibrovac's delicate analysis of sounds in the octet (II, p. 466). In the tercets, Heredia introduces a herdsman (cf. the similar figure in a similar scene in 'L'Oubli') who occasionally drinks from the spring. He has no conscious knowledge of the past and is indifferent to it, but his gesture (l. 11) is seen as linking him with the sacrifices of ancient times, when a bull was beheaded in front of the altar. A mixture of wine, milk and bull's blood was put in a vase and the priest, after tasting it, poured the rest over the victim: this was called *libatio* and the vase *libatorio* (l. 14).

This is the only sonnet in *Les Trophées* where the tercets rhyme CDDCDC.

Le Dieu Hêtre
Les Lettres et les arts, 1 March 1886

The epigraph means: 'to the god of the beech tree'. The Garonne valley was thick with beeches. Heredia supposes the Garumni made coffins in wood: in fact, at that time, they burned or buried their corpses in *dolmens*.

The sonnet is neatly constructed. The first quatrain affords a general picture of the relationship between the beech and the Barbarian: his hut under the tree, the vista of surrounding forest, the beech's living qualities—strength, suppleness, smoothness, whiteness, hardness. The second quatrain amplifies: the forest gives all the Garumni need, shelter, flesh to eat and skins to wear. ('les bêtes qu'il force', in l. 6, is weak padding). The first tercet sums up the rich and happy simplicity of this free life (l. 9: 'sans maître' echoes the 'libre' of l. 5); the living beech is a constant friend. The second tercet provokes the most thought and suggestion. 'Franche' connotes 'free, loyal, sincere'. There is something fine in the cycle of birth, life and death, a sense of continued tradition and accepted inevitability (cf. the implications of the bowed head and the fact that the grand-children know all the time that the beech's main branch will make a good coffin.) The last line is excellent, the position as well as meaning of 'incorruptible' and 'maîtresse' giving them strong affective value, the aura of which spreads over the humans as well.

Aux Montagnes divines
Revue des deux mondes, 1 February 1893

The epigraph is incomplete. In full, it reads: 'Deo garri Geminus Servus V.S.L.M. et pro suis conservis' ('To the god Gar, from the slave Geminus, in fulfilment of a spontaneous vow and for his companions in slavery'). The epigraph was authentic, on a cippus (l. 10) or broken pillar found near the Gar mountain. To enlarge the setting, Heredia replaces the Gar by the Néthou, the highest peak in the Pyrenees, in the range of mountains called the *Maladetta* or *Monts Maudits*. The scene resembles the panorama visible from Superbagnères, not far from Luchon. Bègle (l. 2) is a small French town in the Gironde. Geminus escaped from the *ergastulum* or Roman prison and from the control of the *municipium* (l. 9), a town subject to Roman authority but self-governing.

The apostrophe is meant to inject immediacy and vigour, but like many such examples in early Romantic poetry, it can be found weak and tiresome; name-dropping and impressive lists can become a too easy substitute for original verbal subtlety and suggestion. Once again, the past comes alive in the present. The awesome mountains represent and preserve freedom. Qualifying 'cri', the adjective 'jeté' is, so to speak, left in the air, 'inviolable, immense et pur', graphically to convey the sonnet's main inspiration.

L'Exilée

La Revue bleue, 19 December 1885

The origin of the epigraph is the inscription on a fragment of altar from the old church at Ardiège (l. 2): 'Mont Sabinula Ser V S'. In his *Epigraphie de Luchon* (1880, p. 47), which Heredia consulted, Julien Sacaze first interpreted this: 'aux Montagnes [par] une esclave du nom de Sabinula'. From this and part of the inscription used for 'Aux Montagnes divines', Heredia composes his epigraph. He imagines Sabinula was a patrician lady who had been exiled from her dear Rome and who, though full of nostalgia for the capital in her quiet retirement, yet grew to love her new mountain home. Tenderness and evening often go together for Heredia. The evocation of the sad Sabinula in the first quatrain sets the tone, with her grey hair and halting step, suggested by rhythm as much as idea ('Chaque soir,/à pas lents,/tu viens/t'accouder là'). Grammont argues (p. 284) that the predominant nasals in l. 3 help to express 'la lenteur, la langueur, la mollesse, la nonchalance'.

6. *Flamine*: a Roman priest. The colour contrast is characteristic of Heredia.

9. The Gar mountain does have seven peaks.

LE MOYEN AGE ET LA RENAISSANCE

See the Introduction, p. 16.

Vitrail

La Lecture, 25 September 1892

'L'homme périssable au milieu des choses qui restent: idée presque banale', comments Ibrovac (*Sources*, p. 93) with under-statement. But 'banal' can be seen as the pejorative form of 'universal'. The sonnet induces the sense of awe, history and mystery any spectator may feel in such a scene. Heredia lets us achieve this ourselves by offering no explicit comment, confining himself to the antithetical octet and sestet, the then and the now of which he is so fond (cf., of the sonnets already covered, 'L'Oubli', 'Nessus', 'La Centauresse', 'Le Vœu'): the proud, colourful pomp once alive in this church as the medieval figures prepared to go crusading or hawking; the still, silent, open-eyed and unperceiving figures of stone that the seigneurs and chatelaines have now become. The balanced antithesis of the poem's structure is present on a smaller scale and with symmetrical variation in ll. 7–8 of the second quatrain: 'Vers la plaine ou le bois', first hemistich of l. 7, is where these figures went for 'le vol des hérons' (second hemistich of l. 8), while Byzantium and Acre, (second hemistich of l. 7), were the exotic destinations of the Crusaders ('Partir pour la croisade', first hemistich of l. 8). The poem's evocative power owes much to exact, suggestive detail—the gerfalcons and sakers (large lanner falcons), the shoes with long pointed toes worn in the thirteenth or fourteenth centuries—to the fusion of life and death in 'yeux de pierre' and 'regardent sans voir' and to the blossoming expansion of the climactic, picturesque image which, according to legend, Heredia took ten years to find.

3. *dextre*: old word for 'right hand'.

For this sonnet, Heredia is indebted to Gautier and Leconte de Lisle (see Ibrovac, *Sources*, pp. 93–4).

Epiphanie
Paris-Noël, 1886

Epiphany comes from the Greek word for 'appearance', the appearance, as here, of the child Jesus to the Three Kings. Epiphany or Twelfth Night (6 January) is also known in France as *Jour des rois*. The picture has its colourful exoticism (the camels, the gold, frankincense and myrrh, the negro attendant, the floral pattern of their clothes, l. 8) but it also captures the simple Christian faith of the Middle Ages (ll. 6–7), the humility of the baby Christ and of the kings. The repetition of the names in l. 14 strengthens the sense of naïveté, but it is a controlled repetition, in symmetrically inverse order. The detail in l. 11 is in the same spirit, movingly simple and *vraisemblable* and probably owed, like the inspiration of the whole sonnet, to many a medieval painting of the Adoration of the Magi. Heredia may have noted the detail of l. 11 during his tour of Italy, from Dürer or Gentile da Fabriano's *Adoration*.

10. *chef*: old word for 'head'.

Le Huchier de Nazareth
Le Meuble en France au XVIe siècle, by E. Bonnaffé, J. Rouam, 1887

This is another beautifully illuminated *vieille image*, forming a diptych with 'Epiphanie' and again reflecting the simple faith of the Middle Ages. Most English readers must reach for their dictionaries to understand the technical terms from carpentry (partly inspired by the language and erudite researches of the book in which the sonnet was first published). The poem is worth the effort: the terms' authenticity is self-justifying and they help Heredia to create an original poetry, especially of roughness, hardness and harsh effort in the first quatrain. The 'bon' is important (l. 1): Joseph, Jesus's father, is morally good and a good craftsman, a master carpenter. The second quatrain is in sharp contrast: anticipation of evening's gentle relaxation in the shade of the tree he knows so well that its shadow marks the passage of time for him. The tone is domestic and intimate, in accord with the love, sweetness and quiet dignity of the family life evoked. The tercets bring another, still stronger, antithesis: a tired, sweating Joseph taking a rest (his wiping of the sweat on his brow with the corner of his apron is a further notation conveying unpretentious simplicity) set against a tireless Jesus all light and activity, his halo ('gloire') and the flurry of golden shavings from his busy plane standing out against the dark background. The climax is pictorially resonant, investing a commonplace detail with aesthetic significance—and also with religious and moral significance too, since Jesus will spend all his efforts bringing light to the world.

10. The verb *choir* is appropriate in the context, being archaic French for 'fall'.

The sounds of the poem are part of its beauty: the three mute *e*s in l. 9 which seem to lengthen and soften the line's effect or the harmonious interrelation of nasals in l. 6 and of *o*s in l. 14.

L'Estoc

Revue des deux mondes, 1 February 1893

The sub-title of this sonnet's first publication ('Inventaire du Trésor de l'Alcazar de Ségovie') suggests that the idea of writing it came from the said inventory, of which an extract appeared in *Recherches sur l'orfèvrerie en Espagne au Moyen Age et à la Renaissance* (Quantin, 1879) by Charles Davillier, a friend of Heredia. The sword's maker (l. 9) was a Spanish goldsmith established in Rome.

4. The ox was the heraldic symbol of the Borgias.

5. *Priape*: see p. 13.

12–14. The poet Ariosto was the panegyrist of the Borgias, the poet Sannazar their detractor. As well as the technical and picturesque details of an *objet d'art*, Heredia clearly loves the ringing syllables of a long Spanish name (l. 9) or the historical vistas opened up by the sword and the two famous names forming the climax of the last line: the corrupt and clever politician of the Borgia family, the Renaissance pope Alexander VI and his equally astute and cruel son Caesar Borgia. 'Ce bâton pastoral' (l. 10), with sarcastic resonance, sums up the power of the sword wielded by the Borgia papacy.

Médaille

La Nouvelle Revue, 15 February 1893

This 'medallion' owes almost everything to the book by Charles Yriarte:

Un Condottiere du XVe siècle. Rimini. Etude sur les lettres et les arts à la cour des Malatesta, J. Rothschild, 1882. It contains two hundred sketches, including both sides of various medallions, some with the profile of Sigismundo Pandolpho (the most famous of the Malatesta family), by the fifteenth-century Italian painter, sculptor, engraver and architect Matteo da Pasti (l. 4). Also described in Yriarte's book are several medallions by da Pasti of Isotta, wife of Sigismundo. The latter was a famous leader who took under his control (l. 10) the Romagna (former Italian province governed by the Church), the Marcha (former province of France) and the gulf of Naples. Yriarte writes:

> de tous ces princes du XVe siècle italien, il est peut-être celui qui représente le mieux les tendances d'une époque où, sous la haute culture des premiers temps de la Renaissance, apparaît encore l'homme du Moyen Age avec sa rudesse, sa violence et son caractère (p. 79).

Sigismundo was himself conquered, by love, and became a poet. His wife Isotta was one of the most cultivated women of the age. The temple at Rimini (l. 11) was erected in her honour.

1. *Vicaire*: title given to a public official who was the Emperor's delegate in countries where he did not reside, like Italy. 'Podestà': a magistrate in Italian cities in the twelfth to fourteenth centuries. He had judicial authority and command of troops. In l. 7, Heredia evokes the names of the Ezzelin, podestà of Vicence, Verona and Venice and their successors the Cane, the Galeas (Christian name common to the Visconti and Sforza of Milan) and the Hercules (Christian name of the Esti family who governed Ferrara, Modena and Reggio).

Heredia's inspiration is the ferocity and vigour of a typical Renaissance leader, but he is also drawn by the latter's devotion to art (poetry, sculpture and bronzes) which he himself clearly shows in such a sonnet. The second tercet, taking its image from the medallion on pp. 148–9 of Yriarte's book (the elephant was the emblem of the Malatesta) brilliantly exploits the antithetical combination of delicacy and massive strength.

Suivant Pétrarque

Unpublished before *Les Trophées*, 1893

Imagining a scene like that of Petrarch's actual first meeting with his beloved Laura, Heredia lets the great Renaissance humanist and sonneteer (1304–74) describe the event in a manner resembling Petrarch's own. Thus we perceive Laura's moral qualities, the piety, nobility and modesty Petrarch himself depicted, but also the physical traits Petrarch never forgets, especially her eyes and golden hair. Much of the Italian poet's manner—respectful, submissive, anxious not to offend—and something of his archaic style—e.g. the absence of definite article before *Amour* in

l. 9 or the force of *merci* in l. 11—are captured by Heredia. The final image is prettily climactic, making Heredia's Laura more coquettish than Petrarch's.

Sur le Livre des Amours de Pierre de Ronsard
La Jeune France, 1 September 1883

Ronsard was loved and admired by Heredia (cf. the epigraph to *Les Trophées*, p. 29) and the Parnassians. This tribute to the great sixteenth-century poet embodies a commonplace in Ronsard and the Renaissance generally: the 'then and now' contrast between the fragility of things human and the immortality which art alone can confer. The images too (e.g. 'jardins de Bourgueil', the crown of myrtle and laurel) are Ronsardian.

1. *Bourgueil*: in Anjou, in the Loire country, which Ronsard loved and where he spent his childhood.

3. *Louvre*: the former royal palace in Paris.

9. These three women were celebrated by Ronsard in three collections of poems: *Les Amours de Cassandre* (1552: delicate love poems, mostly decasyllabic sonnets, addressed to a Platonic mistress); *Les Amours de Marie* (1555: more frankly sensual sonnets in alexandrines. Marie came from Bourgueil); *Sonnets pour Hélène* (1578: alexandrine sonnets revealing a grave, restrained sensuality).

La Belle Viole
Revue des deux mondes, 1 February 1893

This tribute to another great figure of the sixteenth-century Pléiade has as its epigraph lines from Du Bellay's famous song of the winnower (*Divers Jeux rustiques et autres œuvres poétiques*, 1558). The dedication has its importance. Heredia's point of departure for his wistful picture was an engraving of a sketch by the sculptor Henry Cros, also entitled *La Belle Viole*, published in the *Revue des deux mondes* on 1 April 1874. It showed in profile a slim, delicate lady in sixteenth-century dress, leaning on a balcony while playing a viola. Below were the lines:

> La Dame qu'a fait vivre à jamais Du Bellay,
> De ses doigts en fuseaux gratte ici la viole,
> Chantant quelque orgueilleuse et rythmique parole
> Echappée à l'amant de bonheur accablé.

Cros and Heredia thus evoke Viole or Viola, anagram of Olive, the name of Du Bellay's poetic Muse (cf. his *L'Olive*, published in 1549) who is singing his winnower's song. Du Bellay is seen as far away in Italy (ll. 1–2, 7–8), sadly missed. 'La douceur Angevine'—concluding words of Du Bellay's famous sonnet from *Les Regrets*, published in 1558, 'Heureux qui, comme Ulysse, a fait un beau voyage'—described his beloved Anjou: Heredia makes him apply them to his lady.

5–8. The euphony is particularly strong here, through the interplay of vowels and alliterated consonants.

Epitaphe

Revue des deux mondes, 1 February 1893

The epigraph has defeated scholars. As far as is known, the French king Henri III (1551–89) did not write verse and certainly wrote none on the death of Louis-Hyacinthe de Maugiron, one of the king's *mignons* or favourites. Maugiron died on 27 April 1578 in a famous duel which he, Quélus (l. 5, who died a month later in the king's arms) and Livarrot fought against three favourites of the duc de Guise (Entragues, Riberac and Chomberg). Many songs and poems were composed about Maugiron's death, including a popular song:

> Seigneur, reçoy en ton giron
> Chomberg, Quélus et Maugiron.

Heredia probably owed something to the *Mémoires-Journaux* of Pierre de l'Estoile: *Journal de Henri III* (1574–80), 1875, in the first volume of which the fancy dress and manners of the *mignons* are well described (cf. second quatrain). Henri III was very fond of Quélus and Maugiron. He kissed their corpses, had their heads shaved and the blond hair preserved. He gave them a superb service when they were buried in the église Saint-Paul (Heredia changes the church to Saint-Germain—for the rhyme?): statues were erected on the magnificent tombs of black marble of which Maugiron's is the sonnet's inspiration.

7. *Myron*: famous Greek sculptor (sixth century B.C.).

8 and 14. The Christian name *Hyacinthe* entails an allusion to the friendship of Apollo for Hyacinth: after the latter's death, Apollo perpetuated his memory by changing him into the flower bearing his name.

Vélin doré

Revue des deux mondes, 1 February 1893

This gilt-edged book of fine parchment, the work of the sixteenth-century binder Clovis Eve, actually belonged to Heredia (see Ibrovac, *Sources,* p. 110). The poet's love of books was physical. He liked to clean and caress them. This tender solicitude is evident here as he dwells on the fading of the gold and of the interlaced design. The larger and historical vista is kept for the sestet's climax; it is evoked with a personal, felt, sensuousness.

10. The three women are Marguerite de Valois (1553–1615, daughter of Henri II and Catherine de Médicis), the famous Mary Stuart (1542–87, wife of François II) and Diane de Poitiers (1499–1566, favourite of Henri II).

La Dogaresse
La Revue des lettres et des arts, 27 October 1867

This Venetian scene is clearly inspired by the paintings of Titian (l. 2) and Veronese. The richly colourful pageantry of the many noblemen in the first eleven lines is set in the climax against the equally exotic but more piquantly intriguing detail of the smiling wife of the doge (chief magistrate in the famous republics of Venice and Genoa).

Sur le Pont-Vieux
Le Livre des sonnets, Lemerre, 1875

There is a fine concentration of contrasted detail in this reconstruction of a scene from the youth of Benvenuto Cellini, the famous Florentine sculptor and engraver (1500–71). Heredia greatly admired Cellini ('le plus merveilleux artiste du monde', as he described him [Ibrovac, i, p. 260]) and knew his writings. Cellini tells in his autobiography that, at the age of fifteen, he became an apprentice in the workshop of the goldsmith Antonio di Sandro (hence the epigraph). The initial contrast is between the two quatrains: in the first, we see di Sandro's ardent devotion to his art as he bends over the inlaid enamel work that dispenses such a feeling of peace, in the second quatrain the Ponte Vecchio in Florence, spanning the river Arno, offers its spectacle of humanity outside the artist's workshop, its jostling motley crowd composed of ordinary citizens ('la cape'), priests ('le froc et le camail') and beautiful Florentine women. In ll. 7–8, with superb succinctness, the reference to the sun continues the progression of time begun in l. 1 and enables Heredia, so to speak, artistically to consecrate the women and the scene with the evocation of the 'ciel de vitrail' and the women's haloes. In the tercets, all the apprentices are distracted by the women, all save the young Cellini whose future greatness is adumbrated by his intense concentration on his engraving. The sonnet's pattern is, by quatrain and tercet, symmetrically ABBA: second quatrain and first tercet depict the bustle and beauty of ordinary humanity and its feelings while the first quatrain and second tercet convey the great artist's singleness of purpose. To cap all, Cellini's engraving is an impressive fusion of the huge (the Titans' struggle) and the tiny (the dagger's handle).

Le Vieil Orfèvre
Recherches sur l'orfèvrerie en Espagne au Moyen Age et à la Renaissance, par le baron Charles Davillier, Quantin, 1879

The art of the goldsmith was closely connected with sculpture and, in the fifteenth century, left works of great merit, nearly all religious (crosses, chalices, monstrances). The four names in l. 2 and the one in l. 13 were all fifteenth- and sixteenth-century master goldsmiths in Spain, mentioned by Davillier in his book, from which Heredia drew his inspiration for the sonnet. If the name-dropping can be tedious for the modern reader, it must be acknowledged that Heredia gives his poem liveliness and movement by making it a direct address from the imagined old goldsmith and by the dramatic contrast between the old man's past delight in the ornamentation of profane subjects and his present desire to save his soul by devoting his last days to fashioning a monstrance.

7. *Saint sur le gril*: an allusion to Saint Laurent, martyred in Rome in 258 A.D.

8. *Danaé surprise*: Danaé, imprisoned in a bronze tower, was loved by Zeus who visited her in the form of a shower of gold (this was her surprise). She later gave birth to Perseus.

Jules Lemaître remarks of this sonnet:

Croyez-vous qu'il soit possible de substituer, sans dommage pour le poème, d'autres rimes à celles-là? Notez d'abord que plusieurs des mots qui sont à la rime sont des mots essentiels du vocabulaire de l'orfèvre et de l'armurier. Mais, en outre, on sent fort bien qu'une rime ouverte en *ère* ou en *ale* si vous voulez, n'eût pas convenu ici, et que l'*i* devait dominer à la fin des vers, voyelle aiguë comme l'épée, menue et fine comme les joyaux. Et sans doute la rime en *rie* (*pierrerie*, *fleurie*, *orfèvrerie*) n'eût point été malséante; mais qui ne voit que la sifflante adoucie qui se joint à la voyelle affilée (*frise*, *irise*) fait rêver de ciselure, de pointe glissante sur un métal? (*Les Contemporains, études et portraits littéraires*, 2ème Série, 1886, p. 58.)

L'Epée

La République des lettres, 14 January 1877

On its first publication, this sonnet was dedicated to Edouard de Beaumont, author of *La Fleur des belles épées* (1885). Julian del Rey (l. 14) was a famous sword-maker of Moorish origin. Heredia's description could have run the risk of being too statically dull. But he makes visual effects arouse feelings: he breathes life into his poem by dwelling on the sword's basic inspiration, its appeal to martial sentiments and the ancient calling of arms (l. 1: 'l'antique chemin'), by making the sonnet an impassioned apostrophe from some mature knight to a young male for whom the priesthood is a possible alternative career (l. 4). A fighting nobleman's nature is needed to appreciate and to be able to wield this weapon (ll. 3–4). The imperative in l. 5 imparts further vigorous immediacy, sustained by the sensations arising from the poetic conceit in the rest of the second quatrain: the Hercules in chased gold on the handle (smooth and well worn—an implicit appeal to the boy's memory of fighting ancestors) warms and flexes his muscles when the handle is gripped—by the right person! The vital words take the stresses—'gonfle', 'splendide', 'muscles de fer', 'surhumain'. The sonnet is punctuated at the beginning of the sestet by a more urgent imperative. The tone is mounting, there is more movement, helped by the *rejets* (ll. 9–10, 10–11, 13–14), as the blade's shimmering sparks come alive. The sword's quivering light communicates a human 'frisson' (l. 11). Its blade is both pliant ('souple') and firm ('solide'). The climax's final conceit, hinging on the ambiguity of 'gorge' (neck of sword and bosom of woman) is perhaps a little forced.

A Claudius Popelin
L'Artiste, 1 February 1868

After considerable success as a painter, Heredia's friend Marcel Claudius Popelin (1825–92) devoted himself to the art of enamelling. Heredia's tribute, with a typical contrast of past and present, links Popelin's achievements with past ancestral artists (the background given by the octet), but the sonnet's emphasis is kept for the sestet, to stress that, by enamelling, Popelin 'a *fixé* son génie au *solide* métal'. Heredia admires the virtues of firm craftsmanship in a hard, well-defined medium that endures.

3–4. The fingers are meant to belong to the 'bourgeois en prières'. In this version they are too near 'les maîtres d'autrefois' and 'de hauts barons'. The first version was clearer:

> Et fait agenouiller des bourgeois en prières
> Entre leurs doigts pieux tournant leurs chapeaux.

Email
La Revue de Paris et de Saint-Pétersbourg, 15 May 1884

This sonnet was inspired by Popelin's enamelling, about which he wrote in *L'Art de l'émail* (1868) and *L'Email des peintres* (1886). The enamelling Popelin helped to revive had reached a high level of achievement and popularity in the Renaissance, linked as it was with engraving and the goldsmith's art. In characteristically dramatic fashion, Heredia enlivens his poem by the direct apostrophe to the enameller, the first quatrain immediately capturing the heat, urgency, effort and attentive care necessary for the art. The rest of the sonnet is decorative illustration, as much on Heredia's part as on the part of the enameller to whom it is imputed. The second quatrain first evokes conventionally dignified themes, then, ll. 7–8, more awesome topics (Hercules fighting the Hydra of Lerna, or a struggle with the mythical hippocampus or sea-horse). The sestet's climax provides Heredia's own suggestion for a subject, fiercely erotic and more grandiose still, a profile of some female warrior aggressively attired.

10. *Ophir*: a mythical Eastern country legendarily rich in gold.

11. All four were Amazons—warlike ladies (from Pontus in Asia Minor) who fought various legendary heroes.

14. *gorgone d'or*: a gold covering for the breast in the shape of one of

the Gorgons (probably Medusa), fabulous sister monsters who turned to stone those who looked upon them.

Rêves d'émail
La Nouvelle Revue, 15 February 1893

This sonnet obviously forms a diptych with 'Email', the previous sonnet, and is equally inspired by Popelin's work. Though the direct address is now from the enameller to us, the poem's structure is very similar to that of 'Email': the first quatrain is all heat and fire, ardour and exaltation as the copper is enamelled, l. 5 succinctly and urgently transmits the birth and development of the enamel work and the rest of the sonnet is again decorative illustration from myth and legend.

1. *l'athanor*: name given in the Middle Ages by the alchemists to the furnace or kiln they used.

7. *Centaures*: see commentary for 'Nessus'. *Pan*: see commentary for 'Pan'. *Sphinx*: see commentary for 'Sphinx'. *la Chimère*: see commentary for 'Le Vase'. *l'Orgie*: see commentary for 'Ariane'.

8. For the three proper names, see commentary for 'Persée et Andromède'.

9. Achilles admired the beauty of Penthesileia, queen of the Amazons (she was mentioned in 'Email'). He mourned over her corpse after he had killed her as an enemy during the siege of Troy.

10. When his wife Eurydice died on their wedding day, Orpheus went down to the Underworld and recovered her on the condition that he did not look back at her until they reached the upper world. Heredia's dramatic picture suggests Orpheus's anguish when he broke the condition and saw Hell's unbreakable gate swing shut. This is a first awesome climax in the first tercet, then we have a quick reference to one of Hercules's tasks (lake Avernus, near Naples, was regarded as the entrance to Hell; Hercules had to go down and bring back Cerberus, the dog that guarded it) and finally a second more sensually horrible climax as Heredia recapitulates the plight of Andromeda (see the commentary for the subsection 'Persée et Andromède').

LES CONQUERANTS

See the Introduction, p. 18.

Les Conquérants
Sonnets et eaux-fortes, Lemerre, 1869

Heredia evokes the departure and voyages, not just of Christopher Columbus in 1492, but of many *conquistadores* of that time. The sonnet opens like a thunderous fanfare: the image of predatory birds leaving their eyrie helps to convey the predominant impression of fierce and awesome endeavour. In the second quatrain, the adventurers' goal is seen as both psychological and geographical. *Cipango* (l. 6) was the name given to rich lands which were thought to exist in the west, near to Cathay (China). The imagination of Spanish and Portuguese explorers was exalted by fantastic ideas of fabulous countries full of gold, like Solomon's Ophir. Thus, having discovered *isla española* (Haïti) and hearing of a province inland called *Cibao*—which sounded like *Cipango* —Columbus set off for Cuba, which he thought was part of Cathay. The explorers believed that Japan had gold mines ('fabuleux métal', l. 5). The trade winds ('vents alizés', l. 7), blowing from N.E. in the Northern hemisphere, tilted their masts towards the New World in the west. The tercets' power of suggestion capitalizes on the octet's background. Only the night-time of the journey is evoked. In the first tercet, it allows the dreams of those who are sleeping to be emphasized and stresses the anti-cipation of dawn and great discoveries, while, in the second tercet, those who are on watch witness the promise symbolized by the climactic rise of stars they have never seen before. The last two lines provoked much correspondence and discussion in 1905 (see Ibrovac, ii, p. 336). If the adventurers are heading west, as Columbus did, they do not cross the equator and therefore cannot see new stars (like the Southern Cross); moreover, since the stars would set in the west, the sailors would see them *going down*. But it has been argued that even on Columbus's voyage, constellations in the southern hemisphere would have been visible even if he did not actually cross the Line or equator. And in any case, Heredia was probably thinking of other journeys like those of Pizarro, leading to the conquest of Peru, when the Line was obviously crossed.

Every rhyme is rich. The quatrains' rhymes in *a* and *ai* are appropri-ately ringing while, in the tercets, the rhymes in *i* or *é* are quieter and more in keeping with the depiction of sleep and dreams.

Jouvence
Le Parnasse contemporain, 1876

Brought up at the court of Aragon, the sixteenth-century Spanish *con-quistador* Juan Ponce de Leon took part in Columbus's second voyage to the New World and in various exploits. In 1512, he set off in search of a new Fountain of Youth which was said to flow in one of the Bahama islands. Despite much effort and suffering, he met with no success. Sailing N.E., he discovered Florida (l. 8). He is seen as dying there; in fact, wounded in Florida, he returned to Cuba to die. The change is for dramatic effect (cf. the image of the old man planting his flag in the ground destined to be his grave). For further effect in the conclusion, Heredia uses direct apostrophe and a competent poetic conceit: this *conquistador* did not find his Fountain of Youth, but Fame gave him immortal youth instead.

Le Tombeau du Conquérant
La Conque, 1 May 1891

Hernando de Soto was among the most famous of the *conquistadores*. He took part in Darien's campaign and went with Pizarro on his expedition to Peru. He died of fever on the banks of the Mississippi he had discovered. To hide his death, his successor Moscoso buried him during the night, but when the Indians noticed the freshly disturbed earth of the grave, Moscoso had the corpse dug up and thrown into the middle of the Mississippi. From this detail, Heredia constructs a poem of firm contrasts, resonantly relevant to its title. De Soto conquered Florida but it conquered him (l. 4). Not for such a conqueror a conventional tomb (first tercet) but the exotic background of wild American landscape (ll. 1–2); not for such a rare man an ordinary grave in the ground, but, untroubled by the Redskin or bear (further exotic detail—revealing the influence of Chateaubriand?), the eternal murmuring moan of the wind in the cypresses beside the wide expanse of the great Mississippi. Once again, immortal Nature is a background and, to some extent, a consoling presence.

5. The vocabulary is heavily literary, some would say pompously platitudinous: 'vil', 'messied', 'trépas'.

Carolo Quinto imperante
Le Parnasse contemporain, 1876

Bartolomé Ruiz was the famous pilot who distinguished himself in the armada of Francisco Pizarro on his 1526 and 1530 expeditions. Ruiz figures in 'Les Conquérants de l'or'. It was Charles V (King of Spain—Castile, l. 9, was Spain's most important kingdom—and Emperor of Germany) who provided help for Pizarro's expeditions. The same king is supposed to have uttered the famous words about the empire on which the sun never sets (cf. l. 11 and title, 'to the Emperor Charles V'). Ruiz was the first to cross the equator. Characteristically, as poet and amateur numismatist, Heredia narrows his perspective very sharply from the first tercet (the wide expanse of the Spanish empire) to the details of the royal crown.

3. *Jardins de la Reine*: name given by Christopher Columbus to the many islands to the south of Cuba because of their agreeable appearance, their rich and varied vegetation.

7. By their singing, the sirens, fabulous monsters half women half fish, lured sailors to destruction on the rocks where they lived.

L'Ancêtre
La Renaissance littéraire et artistique, 24 August 1873

This sonnet and the next three evoke the memory of Heredia's famous ancestor Don Pedro de Heredia, El Adelantado (name formerly given by the Spaniards to the governor of a province). This *conquistador* took part in the expedition to the Indies of Bartholomew Columbus, brother of Christopher. Heredia's poem was inspired by the portrait in enamel by his friend Claudius Popelin (see dedication and the reproduction as frontispiece of Ibrovac, i). The qualities in Don Pedro emphasized by Heredia are traditionally heroic and Spanish: independence, endurance, pride, courage and melancholy.

5. *Côte-Ferme*: *Tierra Firme*, the mainland of South America (as distinct from the islands) and New Spain.

8. Florida was discovered by the Spanish in 1512.

14. *la Castille d'Or*: name given to the region of the Panama isthmus at the time of the conquest of South America, rich in gold mines, prosperous and famous.

A un Fondateur de ville
Le Parnasse contemporain, 1876
See commentary for 'L'Ancêtre'.

Cartagena de las Indias (now in Colombia) was founded by Don Pedro de Heredia in 1532 on a sandy island near the mouth of the river Magdalena; it reminded the explorers of the Spanish town Cartagena. On the Heredia family's escutcheon or coat of arms there is a silver city (Cartagena) in the shadow of a golden palm (cf. ll. 13–14). The sonnet's type of structure and style are by now very familiar: dramatic apostrophe for immediacy, a basic contrast, hinged on l. 8, between past and present, between Don Pedro's ambitious dream and Cartagena's present decay. Once again, eternal forces provide a melancholy and exotic background for transient human endeavour (cf. the climax in the last two lines). The second tercet also implies the power of art, in the coat of arms, to survive.

1. *Ophir*: the legendary country in the East where Solomon sought gold.

11. Heredia patently attempts to pack action and intensity into his line: 'fiévreux', 'dévore'.

This and the two previous sonnets all have their final rhymes in 'd'or', significant for meaning (the rich aura entailed) and sound (ringing, open, sonorous rhyme).

Au Même
L'Ermitage, February, 1893
See 'L'Ancêtre' and 'A un Fondateur de ville'.

The sonnet's structure is again a contrast, between the ephemeral glory gained by other *conquistadores* and Don Pedro's lasting achievement, the founding of a city and the conquest made for Christianity. Heredia thus reverses the viewpoint of the previous sonnet; the sestet's climax highlights the strong durability of the town he founded and, taking up again the image used in ll. 12–14 of the previous sonnet, relates past and present, ancestor and poet.

1. *l'Inca, l'Aztèque, les Hiaquis*: various indigenous South American peoples.

7–8. *Magdalena*: see notes for previous sonnet. The river Atrato runs into the gulf of Darien on the north coast of present Colombia. The name Darien was given to the colony Santa Maria la Antigua, founded by the Spaniards after defeating the Indians in the region.

A une Ville morte
La Revue indépendante, February, 1887
The dates in the epigraph relate to events in the sonnet: in 1532, Cartagena was founded by Don Pedro de Heredia, in 1583 the city was besieged by Drake and occupied by the English (l. 5), in 1697, it was bombarded and taken by the Frenchman François de Pointis (l. 8). For the modern reader especially, this sonnet is one of the best in 'Les Conquérants'. There is scarcely any name-dropping, the strong apostrophe and the contrast between past and present provide a firm structure and enough feeling for a good lyrical synthesis of details, immediately begun in the first line. The dominant impression is of vibrant, exotic and rather grandiose sadness that former glories have to pass away in the perspective of a timeless nature outlasting the doings of man: the tercets convey this impression most cogently, helped by the sounds (cf. the alliteration in *m* in ll. 9–10) and the resonant suggestion of the last line. Baudelaire would have liked this poem and admired its fusion of the radiant and the sombre.

L'ORIENT ET LES TROPIQUES
See the Introduction, p. 19.

LA VISION DE KHEM
All three sonnets in *La Revue du monde nouveau*, 1 April 1874
See the Introduction, p. 20.

I

The first sonnet of the triptych evokes noon in the desert, its desolation, hardness and cruelty. The first quatrain gives a general picture of the Nile sluggishly winding through an Egypt stunned by the blinding heat. Its opening is starkly sudden (cf. the full stop after *Midi*). Simple adjectives are as much affective as strictly informative—'vieux' (l. 2), 'implacable' (l. 4). Following a technique which anticipates the modern cine-camera's progressive shift from a panoramic view to close-ups of particular aspects of a scene, Heredia then pinpoints the sphinxes opposite the needle-like columns. He personifies these symbols of an alien, hieratic culture only to make them even more impersonal ('n'ont jamais baissé la paupière'). In the first tercet, solitude and death are implied by the presence of the vultures (l. 10, *gypaëtes*); one detail of activity serves to emphasize stillness all the more, just as the one black spot of the vultures in the distance enhances the white serenity of the clouds. In l. 11 we are given a powerful recapitulation of the sonnet's whole sense so far, just before we are led into the harshly triumphant climax. Anubis (the Egyptians gave him a man's body and a jackal's head) was the god of burial and embalming and served as a kind of watchdog for a necropolis or city of the dead. The mere mention of 'l'Anubis d'airain' conjures up inscrutable cruelty: this impression is given an ecstatic intensity of barbaric horror by 'chaude joie' and the startling image in the last line's superb oxymoron ('Silencieusement . . . aboie'). Significantly, it is the last word of the sonnet which transmits the surprise.

Khèm: the ancient name of Egypt.

4. *Phré*: one of ancient Egypt's most important gods, later confused with Osiris, symbol of the sun.

II

The dead march again in the tombs of the necropolis where the ancient Egyptians buried their kings. The bodies were embalmed with rich unguents and surrounded by galleries connected with the outside. The galleries had hieroglyphic inscriptions giving details of the dead kings' lives.

The scene outside is set in one line: a heavy, plump, moon accompanied by a distinctive rhythm where the *coupes*—6/5/1—help to make the moon appear suddenly, full, radiant and round, in the consciousness of the reader. With exact, evocative detail, the rest of the first quatrain sets the general scene inside the tombs as the kings awake from their liturgically rigid posture. We are witnessing a re-enactment of the former glories of the Rhamses (l. 5, name common to many kings of ancient Egypt who reigned in Thebes circa 1600 B.C.); their imposing train is evoked with hushed breathlessness (l. 5: 'innombrable et sans bruit'). Gautier had 'la sentinelle granitique' in his 'Nostalgies d'obélisque' (*Emaux et camées*, 1852)—to which Heredia clearly owes much—but the latter's new combination, 'calme granitique' (l. 7)—and, better still, the 'rêve granitique' which it became in later editions of *Les Trophées*—is more lyrically dense with its fusion of spirit and matter and its suggestion of mysterious inflexibility. The retinue has come from the sculptured shapes on the walls of the galleries. The 'Bari' (l. 10) was an Egyptian

boat used to transport the dead. 'Ammon-Ra' (l. 11) was the all-power-
ful Sun God. He is usually depicted with a disc or halo (cf. l. 12) and
often represented with a ram's head (again cf. l. 12). The startling climax
takes the characteristic form of an oxymoron ('S'éveillent . . . éternel
sommeil'). Our impression of hardness and ferocity is heightened by 'se
dressant sur leurs *griffes*'. The rhythm of the last three lines (3/3/6:
3/3/6: 6/6—with strong pauses after the third syllables in ll. 12 and 13) is
calculated to throw emphasis on the comparatively greater 'sweep' of the
last line.

III

This sonnet continues the previous one. The procession swells and the
dark hypogeum or underground chamber is left empty. The Pharaohs
were buried with their servants, ministers and slaves (cf. l. 5: 'Bêtes,
peuples et rois'). They were surrounded by images of animals like the
human-headed sparrow-hawk (l. 4) which was the form taken by the
soul, watching over the corpse and waiting to re-enter it on the day of
resurrection. A *cartouche* (l. 3) was an oval ring containing hieroglyphic
names and titles of Egyptian kings. As in the two previous sonnets,
Heredia infuses dramatic life by his imaginative depiction of the actions
and movements of figures actually dead or merely sculptures on walls.
But the animated figures do not leave behind the marks of their con-
finement in death—cf., in l. 7, the pitch that was applied to the corpses'
lips at burial. The eruditely exotic detail of ll. 5-11 was of a kind calcu-
lated to delight Leconte de Lisle or Flaubert. The gold uraeus (l. 5)—
from a Greek word meaning 'with a tail'—was a representation of the
snake *naja* which adorned the front of the Pharaohs' headdress: it was
the symbol of their divinity. Heredia makes it coil and shimmer. The
gods' names (l. 8) are resolutely esoteric, alien, even barbarous, in both
meaning and sound. 'Hor' or Horus, son of Isis and Osiris, was a solar
god in the shape of a falcon. 'Knoum' was god of cataracts, with a ram's
head. 'Ptah' was father of Apis, god of fire and fecundation, the Egyptian
Vulcan, the one who made the world. 'Neith' was a warlike goddess of
Saïs, represented as carrying a bow and two arrows. 'Hathor' was a cow-
headed goddess of Beauty and Harmony, the Egyptian Aphrodite. The
rest are led by 'Toth Ibiocéphale' (l. 9—*ibiocéphale* means 'with the head
of an ibis', a stork-like bird venerated by the ancient Egyptians). This
god was inventor of writing and secretary to the gods. It was customary
to represent the gods of a district with human bodies and the head of
the animal peculiar to each district. The names of the followers' clothing
could not be more exotic, their dress ('schenti'), their head-gear (the
'pschent', worn only by kings and those gods who reigned over Egypt as
Pharaohs). Before they were walled up, the mummies were covered with
garlands of flowers, blue and white lotuses, and little yellow and red

flowers (cf. l. 11). This weird procession is lent greater eeriness by its setting (l. 12), the rippling insubstantiality of the verb *ondule* (the *u* in *ondule* is expressively repeated in *ruinés* later in the line) and the cold, sinister prolongation of the enormous shadows it casts (cf. l. 14 of 'Némée', for comparable ending and effect).

Le Prisonnier
L'Artiste, 1 February 1868

This brilliantly executed poem follows very closely Gérôme's painting of the same title (cf. the dedication), which was first exhibited in 1863. The subject, most of Heredia's details and the exact positions of the men described are to be found in the painting, a reproduction of which can be seen in Ibrovac, *Sources*, p. 132 (though captious critics would doubtless point out that Gérôme's sheik is so placed, bound and on his back, that he would scarcely be able to see the Nile). The sonnet is constructed with characteristic firmness and clarity. First quatrain: exotic background with agreeable internal rhyme or interplay of sounds (e.g. 'couchant—pourpre', 'd'or—endort', 'frange—plonge—fange'). Second quatrain: differently exotic description of the overseeing master in the bows of the boat, lost in drugged oriental stupor, and the contrasting efforts of the two negro oarsmen in the middle of the boat. Then, in the first tercet, more liveliness and ferocity as we reach the stern where the wild 'Arnaute' (Albanian) is zestfully playing his instrument. Finally, in the second tercet, the surprise and climax as the captive sheik is pictured lying in the middle of the boat, staring vacantly into the Nile. In content and tone, 'Le Prisonnier' is very much in the tradition of Victor Hugo's *Les Orientales* (1829). Thus, like Hugo's poem 'Clair de lune' from that collection, it is predominantly picturesque and visual, totally lacking in 'moral' preoccupation; as in 'Clair de lune', the harsh cruelty at the end receives no comment and is made part of the whole artistic evocation.

1. The muezzins are Mohammedan criers who proclaim the hours of prayer from the minarets of their mosques. These cries have ceased, so that this first detail establishes the time as evening and leads into the first quatrain's other more colourful descriptions.

10. *guzla*: a kind of small one-stringed 'cello. Ibrovac notes (i, p. 281) that, for once, Heredia is inaccurate and unhistorical, putting this Serbian instrument, 'symbole de la tradition chrétienne', in the hands of an Albanian Muslim (the Albanians had been subjugated by the Ottoman Turks in the fifteenth century). Gérôme's painting shows a mandolin.

14. This beautiful line is one of the most quietly suggestive in *Les Trophées*. The exotic word 'minarets' is supported by the words 'pointus' and 'tremblent', both important for sense and position ('pointus' at the end of the first hemistich, 'tremblent' taking a strong accent on the eighth

and ninth syllables), creating the tremulous visual impression which fastidiously crowns the sonnet.

Le Samouraï
La Libre Revue, December 1883

The universal exhibition in 1878 had helped to start a taste for things Japanese which Heredia certainly shared. The Samouraïs were a privileged class of Japanese warriors. Heredia's Samouraï is seen through the adoring eyes of the yearning Japanese lady, who forms part of the first quatrain's brief introduction and setting of the scene. In these few lines, Heredia manages to convey something of the delicacy of Japanese taste ('bambous tressés en fines lattes') and the flatness of the beach on one of the Japanese islands; the musical instrument, the *biva*, augments the exoticism with a touch of authentic local colour. The description of the warrior which forms the major part of the sonnet is an interesting fusion of further exotic, objective details and imaginative penetration of the scene's bizarreness. The Samouraï clad in his hard, gleamingly colourful armour, is likened to one of the crustacea, a crab or lobster. This distances and, so to speak, animalizes him in preparation for the brilliantly accurate climax of the shimmering, quivering antennae on his helmet, yet the warrior remains simultaneously very human for it is love that moves him to adopt the more hurried pace which causes the antennae to tremble. One might claim that, in 1883, imaginatively speaking, Japan was as exotically distant from Paris as the moon now is from all of us on earth. Heredia captures the equivalent of our epoch's American astronaut, bizarrely bedecked, walking on the surface of the moon: in appearance, a strange combination of the human and the inhuman.

8. *Hizen*: maritime province of Japan in the island of Kin-Siev. *Tokungawa*: name of an ancient reigning family in Japan which dominated the class of the Shogun, military governors.

Le Daïmio
Unpublished before *Les Trophées*, 1893

This sonnet and 'Le Samouraï' form a diptych. The daïmios were Japanese warrior princes who came from the class of the Shogun or military governors during the reign of the sovereigns of the Tokungawa family. The rising sun is traditionally associated with Japan. According to legend, in the twelfth century, the powerful Emperor of the Taïra or Heike had one warrior called Kiyomori who became his favourite. It is recounted that, because his master requested it and to show his capacities, Kiyomori opened his fan, held it up and stopped the sun. From then, all the warriors of Heike had on their war fans a red disc representing the sun. 'Le Daïmio' has much in common with 'Le Samouraï': picturesque description of the metallic splendour of a Japanese warrior. But 'Le

Daïmio' is distinguished by its sun-rise which Heredia dramatically relates to the warrior's fan to form a grandiosely colourful first tercet and a significant conclusion in the last three lines.

Fleurs de feu
Le Parnasse contemporain, 1866

The reference in l. 4 to the Chimborazos (the peaks of an extinct volcano in the Andes mountains, in Ecuador) situates this sonnet in the South America Heredia studied with such warm interest. The sonnet's subject, the flowering of the cactus, is given maximum dramatic effect by two main devices. With a typical antithesis between past and present in the octet, Heredia contrasts the flaming eruption that, millenia ago, burst through the crater, with the present silence and stillness of its hard lava. Into this background for the later sestet he injects as much intensity as he can: 'jaillit' (l. 2), 'flamba' (l. 4), 'la cendre pleuvait' (l. 6), 'le sang de la Terre' and 'La lave' (ll. 7–8). The first quatrain's fierce energy prepares us for the presentation of the main theme, the violent flowering of the cactus. Even in the tercets, the subject is dramatically held back until the climactic last line, so that we reach it only after absorbing all the intensive notations in ll. 9–13: the cactus's thunderous explosion is directly linked to the eruption of long ago (cf. l. 9).

Fleur séculaire
Le Parnasse contemporaine, 1876

This sonnet and 'Fleurs de feu' have much in common. They form a diptych and develop a similar theme. Two lines suffice to depict the desolate volcanic background and the rest of the sonnet exploits the dramatic gradualness, before the climax, of the settling of the aloe's seed, its germination and slow absorption of powerful, burning forces until it reaches its gigantic fruition. The explosion of the flowering, with appropriately intensive words ('brûlant', 'embrase', 'géant', 'éclate') is kept for the sestet. Despite its links with the ending of 'Fleurs de feu', the conclusion of 'Fleur séculaire' is rather different: the erotic implications are made more explicit (cf. l. 13—and its blossom is *scarlet*) and the last line's climax is more 'intellectual' than that in 'Fleurs de feu', being an antithetical *pointe* contrasting the hundred years' growth and the one day's flowering. The idea seems definitely to have been taken from Banville's 'Les Affres de l'amour':

> Il est un arbre épars dont la fleur solitaire
> Met cent ans à fleurir et ne dure qu'un jour:
> Elle éclate en s'ouvrant comme un coup de tonnerre.

In 'Fleur séculaire' and the previous sonnet, we see further evidence of the dramatic immediacy to which Heredia was drawn—here, the building-up of tension to an explosive release.

3. *Gualatieri*: volcanic peak in the Andes on the borders of southern Peru and Bolivia.

4. This line is memorable for its internal rhyme, its insistent nasals ('frêle', 'plante', 'rampe') the interplay of *r*s and, slightly, *l*s and the movement implied by the unusual rhythm given by the *coupes*: 2/2/2/1/4/1.

We have seen proof enough of Heredia's taste for rare, rich rhymes (e.g. 'glabre—cinabre' in 'Le Daïmio') but even when the rhymes are *banales*, as here in 'amour-jour' (ll. 13–14), the poem's impact, when read, is enough to carry us over them and even to cause us not to notice.

Only two other sonnets in *Les Trophées* ('A Claudius Popelin' and 'La Vision de Khèm III') have tercets rhyming like those in 'Fleur séculaire': CDCDEE. All three sonnets were composed before 1876.

Le Récif de corail
Paris moderne, 15 January 1882

This famous and much anthologized sonnet gives a brilliantly evocative picture of a tropical under-water scene in the Pacific Ocean. Its structure is simple: in the octet, the fauna and flora beneath the surface, a background for the more dramatic description in the sestet of the fish or shark prowling in the foreground. Heredia again exploits his sense of perspective. For many English readers, the octet's vocabulary presents more difficulty than the sestet's. Heredia creates interestingly new resonances from his use of authentic *mots justes* or exact terms, names of fauna (*oursins*, *madrépores*), 'scientific' or chemical terms (*iode*, *flore*, *vermiculé*).

The predominant impression is of teeming life unfamiliar to humans ('la bête épanouie et la vivante flore'), partly lit up from above—not fully, hence the suggestive 'mystérieuse aurore'—with the close wavy markings of the madrepores providing a pale background for the contrastingly richer, darker hues of the moss, seaweed, the sea-anemones and the sea-hedgehogs. Heredia's coral reef is a feast for the eyes and a miracle of poetic compression. The contrast of light and shade is continued in the first line of the sestet as the fish or shark swims from brighter water (*émaux* is a long-standing cliché in poetry for bright hues) to an area that is appropriately darker, in keeping with the strongly affective l. 11, when the nasals reinforce the sense of slow, lazy, but sombrely menacing power. The sonnet ends with yet another double contrast: from slow prowling to a quick flick of the fish's fin, from shadow to a spread of rich colour occasioned by that movement. No sonnet in *Les Trophées* ends more boldly on a concentratedly visual impression. The syntax and rhythm of the sestet are part of its sense and effect; ll. 9 and 10 lead into l. 11—with a strong pause at the end of l. 11 preparing for the climax—just as ll. 12 and 13 lead into the final line.

'Le Récif de corail' will serve as another instance of those sonnets which reveal a patchwork of probable influences. The title and theme doubtless owe something to Charles Darwin's *Les Récifs de corail, leur structure et leur distribution* (translated by L. Cosserat, 1878), which was in Heredia's library. Darwin notes where coral reefs are found, including Cuba and Abyssinia (cf. 'abyssins', l. 2). Heredia must have kept many memories of tropical fauna and flora, as well as of coral reefs, from his childhood spent in Cuba. From Ibrovac (*Sources*, pp. 137-9) we can note some apparently cogent literary filiations, especially with Sully Prudhomme's sonnet 'Dans l'abîme' (*Les Epreuves*): 'Mystérieux printemps, Eden multicolore', where there glide

> . . . d'innombrables rôdeurs
> Dans les enlacements d'une vivante flore,
> Et sous un jour voilé comme une pâle madrépore.

The rhymes 'rôde-émeraude' are in Hugo ('La Captive' in *Les Orientales*) and Banville ('Le Livre d'heures de la châtelaine' in *Les Cariatides*). The three colours in Heredia's last line recall a line from Leconte de Lisle's 'Bhagavat' (*Poèmes antiques*): 'Et mille mouches d'or, d'azur et d'émeraude'.

However many previous poems lie, absorbed by Heredia, behind 'Le Récif de corail', nothing of this kind can be seen as diminishing its beautiful vision and composition.

LA NATURE ET LE REVE

See the Introduction, p. 21.

Médaille antique
Revue des deux mondes, 1 January 1888
An ancient medallion, in the form of a coin, is the point of departure for a reflection dear for centuries to many poets: all things are doomed to die but art—here, in metal—prolongs their life most of all. The idea was a key one for the Parnassian poets. Gautier's poem 'L'Art' gave it most notable expression. Time is basic to the theme and to the sonnet's structure, which develops from the interwoven contrasts of past and present: ll. 1-2, present; ll. 3-4, past beauty which is lost; ll. 5-8, Sicily's past and history over the years; ll. 9-11, the past is gone, everything dies; ll. 12-14, triumphant climax—the beauty of Sicily's virgins of long ago is preserved in the present by the conquest made over time by the 'médaille antique'.

1. *Etna*: the famous volcano on the eastern slopes of the island of Sicily.

2. *l'Erigone*: in mythology, the daughter of king Icarius, who lived in Attica. Dionysus (Bacchus), grateful for Icarius's hospitality, taught him

the art of making wine. When Icarius gave wine to the people, they took their intoxication for poisoning and killed him. When she found his corpse, Erigone hanged herself from grief. Theocritus was a famous Greek poet, born in Syracuse about 310 or 300 B.C. He composed idylls or pastoral poetry.

5–8. As Ibrovac observes, 'l'histoire d'un pays s'est merveilleusement ramassée dans une strophe' (ii, p. 419). Arethusa is the name of various nymphs in Greek mythology. Best known is the one associated with the Arethusa spring on the island of Ortygia near Syracuse, in Sicily. Arethusa was one of Diana's nymphs. When bathing in the river Alpheios, she was surprised and pursued by the river god as far as Ortygia. It was Diana who saved her by transforming her into a spring. Since the river god Alpheios never succeeded in muddying her waters, Arethusa's myth stood as a symbol that purity can preserve itself without stain even in the middle of danger. She was worshipped in Syracuse and her effigy was on various coins. This fact and the myth of purity explain the relevance of the reference here. Arethusa's purity—and the purity of her profile on coins—was lost when the Roman Empire fell and Sicily was invaded, first by the Saracens in 800 A.D., and then by the Norman Roger Guiscard in 1060: the union of Muslim Saracens and Christian Normans was symbolized in the currency, some coins bearing the stamp of Christ, others that of Mohammed, and some both. By later royal marriage, Sicily passed to France and the House of Anjou dominated the island. Independence was wrested by the island in 1282. Heredia's quatrain presupposes a passing knowledge of this historical perspective.

9. The mute *e*s and the full stops help to lengthen the line and strengthen the predominant tone of restrained emotion and quiet, elegiac melancholy. The line is a trimeter, that is, it is divided into three units: this reinforces the line's function as a kind of reflective conclusion.

10. *Agrigente*: ancient town in Sicily.

Les Funérailles
L'Artiste, 1 February 1868

The contrast here is between past and present, reality and dream, the lives of great warriors and Heredia's own. The rare *je* appears boldly in the sestet: this is the nearest Heredia comes to direct personal confession. The Greek heroes enjoyed the splendour of a glorious death, all Greece mourned them, even the sea lamented their passing (l. 8). Heredia's life will not be cut short, he will die and be buried in the normal, humdrum fashion of an unheroic age. Yet he has dreamed of falling bravely in action like his ancestors (see 'Les Conquérants').

1–2. *La Phocide*: part of ancient Greece crossed by the range of Mount Parnassus. One of its principal towns was Pytho, the older name for

Delphos, with its temple of Apollo, near which was the famous oracle where the priestess, seated on a tripod, pronounced the predictions of the god she served.

8. *la mer de Salamine*: the name belongs to an island in the gulf of Athens, separated from Attica by a narrow stretch of water.

11. *païra*: that is, 'payera'.

Vendange
La Renaissance littéraire et artistique, 28 September 1872

The perspective is again historical as Heredia contrasts the present with the past. The harvesting of the grapes in a contemporary countryside (ll. 1–4) reminds him of the ancient Bacchanalia on the island of Naxos in the Greek archipelago (ll. 5–8), when Ariadne (l. 7, 'la Crétoise', since she came from the island of Crete) succumbed to Dionysus/Bacchus (l. 8, 'le beau Dompteur'): the relationship between Ariadne and Bacchus was treated by Heredia in the sonnet 'Ariane' (see commentary to that poem), beside which 'Vendange' appeared in the *Parnasse contemporain* of 1876. In the Bacchanalia, the oxen and other animals were adorned with young vine-branches, emblems of the god of wine and vines. Dionysus/Bacchus no longer exists for nineteenth-century man, but nature in the form of autumn takes over his role (second tercet).

La Sieste
Le Parnasse contemporain, 1876

A very personal poem by Heredia's standards, describing one of the wooded scenes where he delighted to lie, muse and sometimes compose. The presence of the blazing sun—beloved of Leconte de Lisle and, less, of Heredia himself—is discreetly noted but its rays can only filter through the foliage of 'le dôme obscur' of trees: it is in temperate France that the scene is set, possibly in Brittany, perhaps much further south. The immediately pleasurable associations of a siesta, the warmth and yet refreshing shade of the forest interior, the interplay of light and shadow, the fluidity of the impressions described, all these fundamentally impersonal traits are given more particularly human significance by the climax to which they lead with the second tercet's beautifully poetic conceit. Before we become conscious of the last line's full meaning, the novelty of 'dreams' being 'imprisoned'—with the fusion of the diffusely abstract and the more concretely restricting—is working on our imagination, while 'chasseur harmonieux' is no less arrestingly original. Heredia is constantly searching for the harmony he can find in the nature around him and for its adequate expression in the harmony of his poetry.

LA MER DE BRETAGNE

See the Introduction, p. 22.

Un Peintre

Le Figaro, 12 July 1891

The sonnet is dedicated to Emmanuel Lansyer (all ten sonnets of this Breton cycle were later dedicated to him) and it is about him. Lansyer was a painter of landscapes and seascapes, preferring Brittany for his subjects and especially the west coast and Douarnenez. We have repeatedly witnessed the art with which Heredia concentrates our attention on the most characteristic and significant traits of a scene or event. Here, he pinpoints the Celtic yearnings of 'la race aux yeux pensifs' (l. 1), their struggle to live (l. 2), the subdued light and colours that characterize the long stretches of moorland in that corner of France famous for its ancient crumbling manors and legends. Brittany's beauty entails a certain roughness, the grave attraction of huge vistas of sea that can turn tempestuous. This sonnet is a tribute from artist to artist. Heredia admires the genius of a painter who has understood the soul of a country, who, in the narrow compass of a canvas (ll. 12–13), can capture all that Brittany holds with the openness of expansive suggestion inherent in Heredia's own image in the last line.

Bretagne

La Muse orientale, 15 October 1877

The poem was initially dedicated to Lansyer and entitled 'Arvor' (cf. l. 4). As we shall see in a later sonnet, *ar mor*, in Breton, means 'the sea'. But the case of *ar vor* is more complicated. Words in the Breton language undergo consonant changes in certain circumstances. After certain words, the first consonant of a following word may be modified when the word is feminine. Thus *kêr* means 'house, town' while *ar gêr* means 'the house or the town'. The word *mor* is masculine so in *ar mor*, 'the sea', there is no consonant change. But there also exists the preposition *war*, meaning 'on', which provokes a consonant change whatever the gender of the following noun. *War* has the form *àr* in *vannetais*, the dialect current in the area around Vannes. So, in the Vannes dialect, *àr vor* means 'on the sea, at sea'. But the word is clearly used to carry the same meaning as *ar mor*, that is, 'Brittany' or 'the coast of Brittany': the use of *ar vor* in this way gives the impression that the person first employing it so had only imprecise knowledge of Breton and its consonant changes.

Celebrating qualities of Brittany seen in 'Un Peintre', the present sonnet first expresses the invigorating appeal of salt air and wild waves, the first quatrain ending on a visual impression with a strongly incantatory line which closes on the ecstatic emphases of repeated nasals (l. 4, 'mer blanche arrose'). The visual appeal is extended in the second quatrain (the beauty of the gorse in bloom and the pink heather) and the folklore for which Brittany is famous receives its first allusion for the octet to end on the firmly conclusive and very generalizing eighth line. In the sestet, the personal apostrophe (to Lansyer) which structured the octet is now developed with more urgency as Brittany's heroic past and mythological tradition are briefly evoked before Heredia leads us into a typical climax which is grave, reflectively sad, yet not without consolatory pleasure ('Bercera').

11. *Le menhir*: megalithic monument, viz. a large upright stone.

13. The town of *Is* is supposed to have been situated opposite Douarnenez. It is usually referred to as a legendary town, but traces of Roman roads recently discovered are thought to have met out at sea, in the bay. Perhaps the town did exist and vanished in a cataclysm. In the time of good king Gradlon, around the sixth century A.D., Is was the capital of *la Cornouaille*, a former kingdom and then a duchy of what we know as Brittany. The town of Is was protected from the open sea by a dike: king Gradlon always kept on him, on a necklace round his neck, the golden key that opened the lock-gates. His daughter, the beautiful Dahut, who led a life of debauchery, met the devil in the shape of a handsome young man who, as proof of her love, asked her to take the golden key from her father while he was sleeping so that the sea could be let in. Dahut complied and the waters poured in. Gradlon fled on horseback, Dahut riding pillion. But his horse slackened its pace and the waters were about to engulf Gradlon when a voice from heaven bade him, if he wished to be saved, to abandon to the sea the demon he was carrying behind him. The king obeyed and Dahut perished. But Is was destroyed. Heredia thus briefly evokes the awesome past of the city beneath the sea. His adjective, *voluptueuse*, is well chosen: Is, in Brittany and in Breton, is synonymous with luxurious and dissolute life.

Unlike Is, *Occismor* does designate a geographical reality, the island of Ouessant. The word is learned and synthetic; it is not known who invented it from a basis of authentic Celtic elements. In Breton, *Ouessant* is *Eussa*. Etymologically, *Eussa* means 'the highest/greatest island', which in fact it is, compared with islands nearby. So Heredia's adjective *grande* is as well chosen as *voluptueuse* is for Is. To *Eussa*, the Breton name for the island, gallicised as *Occis* (under the influence of *Occident*?) there has been added the suffix *-mor*, which means 'great', 'enormous', 'magnificent'. So *Occismor* is a pleonastic form, in which the idea of greatness is expressed twice. The approaches to the island of Ouessant are known to be dangerous; this bad reputation is partly owed to its name, since *Eussa* has been linked—wrongly, if one is concerned with linguistic accuracy—with *Euz* ('terror' or 'fright'): hence the saying *Qui voit Ouessant voit son sang*. The name and the place, set in Brittany, land of soulful mystery, were calculated to fascinate.

Floridum Mare

Le Figaro, 12 July 1891

According to one of Heredia's friends (see Ibrovac, i, p. 235), this son-net was composed on the beach at Douarnenez. It is a most subtle and colourful fusion of landscape and seascape (cf. the meaning of the title: 'the sea in bloom'). The first quatrain depicts the land and its harvest, but in sea terms ('roule', 'ondule', 'déferle'); the harrow is seen expli-citly as resembling a bowsprit on a tossing ship. Contrariwise, the second quatrain's theme is the sea, but it is a spread of green to the horizon, like a great meadow, and covered with *moutons* (the ambiguity is very im-portant here: 'sheep' and 'white horses' at sea). The sestet carries further the connection between sea and land. In the first tercet, the gulls are exultantly following the tide in towards the 'swell' (l. 10, *houle*) of the field's ripe corn while, in the second tercet, the land's honeyed breeze is scattering butterflies over 'l'Océan fleuri' ('fleuri' meaning 'in bloom'). Land and sea are mingled in a harmony of changing light, colour and movement lit by the rays of the setting sun. The colour green predomi-nates but the accumulation of adjectives of colour in ll. 5–8 points up the variety. Man is absent from this picture of immense nature or, if present, (working the harrow?, l. 3), overwhelmed. The last line is very lightly, delicately, climactic—perhaps too 'pretty-pretty' for some tastes.

The sounds in this poem would be worth analysing at length: the many labial and dental consonants in the first quatrain, the pleasure of the succession of sounds in 'Roule, ondule' (where 'ondule' partly re-peats 'roule', with an exquisite modulation). Ibrovac is boldly affirmative about the relation between sound and meaning in ll. 2 and 10:

Sourd d'abord (*rou*), le bruit monte (*on*) et s'épand (*ule*), pour finir dans un bruissement prolongé (*fr, erce*) où l'on sent les épis qui bou-gent. Du large, ce dernier son n'est plus perceptible; le bruit plus uniforme correspond à un grand mouvement d'ensemble:

(Vers les blés mûrs que) gonfle une houle dorée;

il n'y a là que trois temps nettement définis: élancement (*on*), point culminant (*ou*), épanouissement (*ée*). (Ibrovac, ii, pp. 364–5.)

Soleil couchant

La Revue des lettres et des arts, 16 February 1868

Yet another scene at sunset, Heredia's favourite time of day if one judges by *Les Trophées*. Once again, the impressions are predominantly pictorial though there is implicit an attitude of wonder and contentment. The onlooker/poet is savouring the varied sounds and sights of the closing day, recapitulating the beauty of Brittany but aware of the hard and even harsh reality of life there (l. 1, 'granit'; l. 2, 'l'*âpre* sommet'). In musical terms, 'Soleil couchant' is a *largo*, alternating sound and silence (ll. 5–11), bringing together man and nature (ll. 7–8) in a sweeping synthesis. The *alors* in l. 9 prepares us for the climax to come: against a dark background (we note the resonantly slow heaviness of l. 12, with its several nasals), the self-conscious grandeur of a colourful sunset.

5 has two features worthy of note: its quiet *es*, which, with the full stop, appropriately slow up the line, its internal rhyme (in *i*) and its alliteration of *s* and *l* sounds.

Maris Stella

Le Semeur, 10 March 1888

The Star of the Sea (cf. title), the Holy Star (cf. l. 11), the Sailors' Star dominates this simple picture of peasant life as it once was on the Brittany coast. The women belonging to the fishermen who have sailed north are praying for their loved ones' safety at sea; Heredia's details are authentic and have strong visual appeal—the peasant caps, the rough, stiff wool and thin cotton cambric that poverty entails for these wives, mothers, daughters and sweethearts on their knees, arms folded, on the slopes of the quayside looking out to sea. Danger is graphically suggested by the image in l. 4, of the waves dashing against the 'île de Batz', a large rock just off the coast at Roscoff. This is a close-knit community as the anxious scene and the names of local Breton towns imply.

8 fulfils its frequent function in Heredia's sonnets, to conclude, draw out with force and emotion the octet's main preoccupation. The octet is not then just a picture, since it opens up perspectives of the life led by the fishermen and their families—their closeness to nature, the inevitability for them of death, the simplicity of their lives and thoughts, their natural piety. The power of religion is perhaps greater still in the sestet: their prayers ascend while the angelus bows their heads and envelops a whole district with all the churches ringing it out. The climax is artistically satisfying, finishing the poem in the expanse of the sky, implying eternity and the God to whom they are praying. The *coupes* in l. 14 (3/1/2/6) with its three well chosen verbs help to give the impression of the gusty wind picking up the sound and spreading it until it dies away in the sky with a sad grandeur.

12. *l'Angélus*: devotional exercise commemorating the incarnation of Christ, said by Roman Catholics at morning, noon and sunset, at the sound of the bell.

Le Bain

La Revue félibréenne, January–February, 1888

Pictorial effect and strong feeling are inseparable here. As the Breton astride his stallion enters the sea, we share the exhilaration of naked freedom amid the golden spray. The second quatrain exploits more intensely impressions similar to those already associated with the seaside in Brittany (cf. 'Bretagne'): invigorating salt air and the exciting shock on the skin of icy water. Several traits recall some of the sonnets in 'La Grèce et la Sicile': stallion and rider are compared to the centaur (l. 1); l. 7 provides a harsh juxtaposition of the human and the bestial ('la chair et le crin') reminiscent of, say, 'Némée' or 'Bacchanale'; the rider is a 'dompteur' (cf. first line of 'Némée'); l. 8 recalls l. 4 of 'Nessus'; above all, the inspiration of some sonnets in 'La Grèce et la Sicile' is present in the vibrant energy released by the sestet's evocation of man and horse fiercely breasting the stinging, fuming foam. Sounds and rhythms play an important part in 'Le Bain'. In ll. 9–10, the hiatuses ('L*a hou*le', '. . . Lui cr*ie. I*l hennit') and full stops, the strident effect of the internal rhymes in *i* ('L*u*i cr*ie. Il* . . .') seem to prolong the sounds from man and horse and infuse them with excitement or fear, while l. 14's four *é*s, its repeated *f*s and *u*s, are part of the energy it evokes. Heredia's plastic sense is again shown in the strong grasp of outlines (l. 4).

Blason céleste
Le Parnasse contemporain, 1876

The profusion of technical terms from heraldry makes this sonnet one of the most imaginatively esoteric in *Les Trophées.* Yet its basic inspiration is simple. As Heredia explains in his first quatrain, he has sometimes seen dazzling, many-coloured clouds at sunset as an immense escutcheon or coat of arms. The rest of the sonnet develops this initial vision: as 'crest' and 'supporters', there are the various heraldic beasts, unicorn, leopard, spread eaglet and serpent devouring a babe, rearing up their huge stature into the heavens, yet, since they are only clouds, these giant monsters, temporarily captive, can be released and dispersed by a gust of wind. The sestet introduces another poetic conceit: in the aerial battles between seraphim and archangels, the escutcheon described must have been won by some celestial baron since, like those of the Crusaders who took Constantinople, it bears the image of the sun against a green background.

9. *certe*: by a poetic tradition and convention, the *s* in this word can be omitted to make one less syllable in the line.

13. The proper names recall the famous St. George and the Archangel Michael.

14. *besant*: a gold coin which became current in Europe at the time of the Crusades, also a heraldic term for a disk. *Sinople*: one of the heraldic enamels (green).

Armor
L'Artiste, 1 February 1868

Ar mor, in Breton, means 'the sea'. Geographically, it also designates the coast of Brittany. It included the major part of *Armorica*, which was the name given to the west coast of Gaul from the mouth of the Seine to the mouth of the Loire. The tribes in this region were called *Armoricans* and later the name *Armorica* was given to the province of Brittany. One of the octet's main functions is to introduce the sestet: its opening is familiar and conversational, the hairiness of the shepherd guide, the 'arome sauvage' and 'l'âpre terre kymrique' picking out details that reveal the roughness and wildness already ascribed to Brittany in previous sonnets. The 'souffle amer' in l. 6 and the quaint presentation by the guide in l. 8, the vigour, violence and immensity of the first tercet are Heredia's characteristic means of heralding and at the same time holding back for greater effect the climax that comes in the second tercet with the full view of the open sea beneath the sombre advance of evening and the intoxicating impact of wind and space. It is worth noting how, when so much else is being created in the narrow confines of the sonnet, Heredia contrives to introduce the characteristic Breton details already noted— 'le genêt d'or', 'le morne paysage', 'la bruyère rose', 'granit noir'.

1. *Raz*: cape in the Atlantic, at the far west of the present *département* of Finistère.

2. *Evhage*: *euagés* is an adjective of Greek origin meaning 'pious' or 'holy'. Ammianus Marcellinus, a Latin historian of the fourth century A.D., refers to *euhages*, a grade of Gaulish bard or druid. So the term may convey a grade of Celtic druid or bard, who would traditionally have worn his hair long (cf. Heredia's adjective *chevelu*). And Stephanos of Byzantium, in the sixth century A.D., refers to a shepherd *Euagés*, who was illiterate but a good comic poet. For evocative purposes in the eyes of a post-Romantic French poet of the nineteenth century, a shepherd can look like a holy man or bearded prophet.

4. *kymrique*: Cymric, Breton, Welsh, one of the peoples akin to the ancient Galli (Welsh, Bretons, Cornish, Irish, Manx, Gaels).

8. *Senèz Ar-mor. Ar mor*, we have seen, literally means 'the sea'. The word *senèz* belongs to literary Breton. It derives from the latin *senat(um)* and means 'synod' or 'senate'. The word is not known in popular Breton and one wonders what it is doing in the mouth of Heredia's long-haired shepherd. *Senèz ar-mor* must literally mean 'the synod, the senate, of the sea'. What are we supposed to understand by this? A more or less solemn meeting of sea-gods? It seems that what knowledge Heredia had of Breton was acquired from books (though he spent many holidays in Brittany). Perhaps, in his reading, he came across *senèz ar mor* and incorporated the words in his sonnet meaning them to signify, as they seem to do, 'Behold the sea! Here is the sea!'

Mer montante
La Conférence La Bruyère, 1862–3 (very different from the present version)

The details of the storm are cogent enough, the solitary gulls carried aimlessly by the wind into which they are flying suggesting the desolation of the rain-drenched coast. The words conveying movement ('s'éparpillant', 'empanachent', 'ruisselants') in ll. 5–8 are varied and energetic. The sestet rises above description to become confession. The dismal scene induces gloomy thoughts and bitter memories, yet the ending is sombrely consolatory: the sea's roar is 'une voix fraternelle', nature and man at least have each other as, together, they send up to the gods above their cries that are never answered.

2. *Raz*: see l. 1 of previous sonnet, 'Armor'. The *pointe de Penmarc'h* is a cape, very rocky like all capes in Brittany, a vast peninsula of granite cut away by the sea and strewn with islands. Ibrovac (ii, p. 473) argues that l. 13 'renvoie le triple écho du bruit des vagues (*-ar, -eur, -or, -er*)'. Imitative or not, the effect is pleasurably mournful.

Brise marine
La Lecture, 25 September 1892
A late sonnet and a fine one, revealing the maturity of Heredia's art. Ibrovac (i, p. 237) understandably wonders why it was not put at the end of 'Les Conquérants', where Heredia had already allowed himself a personal, nostalgic, tone. It is the only real evocation in *Les Trophées* of Heredia's native island, Cuba, and in a happy antithesis which unites that island he had loved with the country and province which became so dear to him. The first quatrain's Breton setting is by now familiar: rocky headland with heath, probably the Pointe du Raz on the coast near Douarnenez. The mournful aspect of the scene is built up by several words: 'défleuri', 'mort', 'uniformément grise', 'fané', 'pend', 'dernier'. As for its rhythm, the symmetry of l. 1 (2/4/2/4) helps to suggest the landscape's monotony. The strong pause at the full stop in l. 2 gives a sombre simplicity to the detached sentence of three words. In l. 3, the long movement of eleven syllables stops at the monosyllable 'brise' as the wave breaks on the shore. Terms of smell dominate the second quatrain ('arome', 'exhalé', 'effluve', 'souffle', 'parfumé') where the warm exhalation contrasts with the implied coldness of ll. 1–4 and the exotic quality of 'parfumé' with the bareness of the Breton landscape. Line 7's incipient nostalgia prepares us for the sestet as does the very form of l. 8, whose question is to be answered. Rhythmically speaking, the long flow of ll. 5–7 is conducive to the impression of a gradual exhalation by the sea and a slow breathing-in by the poet, a reflective musing on the perfume. The first tercet's cry of recognition is an animating and refreshing break in the rhythm before the evocation of the perfume's origin—the blue West Indies, with their ecstatic heat. Line 11's *a* sounds, with its meaning, help to slow up the rhythm again prior to the second tercet's olfactory impression which imaginatively and

nostalgically links the two countries so different in nature and so separated in space.

The sonnet's construction is admirable. Quatrains and tercets are balanced, the first quatrain and first tercet giving visual impressions, the second quatrain and second tercet olfactory impressions. And there is a contrast between the vision in the first quatrain and that in the first tercet. The second tercet's construction is especially interesting: the words beginning the three lines form a main sentence ('Et j'ai respiré la fleur . . .') which is interrupted by two interpolated clauses, thus giving importance to the initial words and reflective body to the whole sentence. The last line's five rhythmic accents ('*fleur*', 'ja*dis*', '*éclose*', 'jard*in*', 'Amé*rique*') also slow it up and make it more climactic. The sestet's image can be taken literally, but Heredia is evoking childhood memories.

All the rhymes are rich except 'lieues-bleues' and 'courtil-pistil'; the latter are rich only for the eye since the *l* of 'pistil' is pronounced, the *l* of 'courtil' is not. There is no fault in repeating the rhymes *grise* and *brise*, since the repetitions are different parts of speech with different meanings. The rhyme pattern shows a piquant and appropriate contrast like the one between the two countries: the quatrains are in *i*, short and long, which has suggestions of delicacy and musing subtlety, while the 'occidental-natal' in the tercets is a more ringing rhyme, in keeping with the sense's stronger affirmation. Even 'kymrique-Amérique' is harder.

La Conque

Le Parnasse contemporain, 1866

This apostrophe to a sea-shell is built on a simple comparison. After being rolled for years over vast distances by the turbulent seas, the shell has come to rest in quiet sand; but it cannot forget the mournful, despairing cry of the open seas. The poet, too, though now in a quiet haven, cannot forget the stormy emotion he once experienced on account of 'Elle'. The feminine is mysterious. It could, with some straining, be interpreted as referring to 'clameur', the noise of the sea in Heredia's native Cuba. But the capital letter seems to indicate some young woman loved in Heredia's youth. Ibrovac (ii, p. 495) has a nice formula: 'la clameur de la mer répond à l'orage du coeur', but he is unimpressed. He thinks that the first eleven lines lead us to expect 'une plainte immémoriale devant le mystère de l'existence' (ii, p. 394) and that the reduction to 'un sentiment individuel' is disappointing. Though the poem is not one of Heredia's best, this judgement seems harsh for the octet is competently imaginative, l. 11 full of original suggestion, the whole sonnet resonantly affective in a conventionally 'Romantic' manner. On the other hand, Ibrovac defends Heredia, albeit very cautiously, against Grammont's condemnation of the hiatus in l. 9 ('Mon âme est deven*ue* *une* prison sonore'), since the two *us*, 'désagréables en soi, sont comme un écho de la "lointaine rumeur" et peuvent avoir leur valeur dans une description de la conque' (p. 460).

Le Lit

Le Meuble en France au XVIe siècle, by Edmond Bonnaffé, J. Rouam, 1887 This sonnet seems really to belong to 'Le Moyen Age et la Renaissance'. It owes much to Bonnaffé's book (see Ibrovac, *Sources*, p. 154). An object prosaic enough in itself becomes a symbol of man's attachment to tradition and the virtues of family life. The many antitheses give the poem body and structure (e.g. 'Triste . . . joyeux', 'Enfant, époux', 'Funèbre ou nuptial', etc.) and the concluding reflection has something of the massively comforting appeal of the bed itself. It would be unfair to criticize 'Le Lit' merely because its values are more alien to those of our time than to those of Heredia's. But the poem entails such reference to every kind of bed and its various functions, its aim is so essential and general that Heredia is led into many heavy platitudes. His art is very different from, say, Rimbaud's, yet at its best it is as good in its way. But one would not choose 'Le Lit' to illustrate Heredia's best art.

Grammont and Ibrovac have an interesting difference of opinion about ll. 9–10. Grammont argues (p. 315) that

si l'accumulation des labiales est trop considérable elles frappent forcément l'attention et le vers est mauvais quand l'idée qu'il exprime ne s'accommode pas de cette répétition:

> Humble, rus*ti*que et *c*los, ou *f*ier du *p*avillon
> Triom*ph*alement *p*eint d'or et de *v*ermillon

le premier hémistiche peindrait parfaitement les gambades d'une chèvre, et le reste le plus dédaigneux mépris (p. 315).

Ibrovac respectfully—or ironically?—comes to the rescue of Heredia:

M. Grammont ne peut pas avoir tort, mais il nous semble qu'il n'a raison qu'à moitié: il ne tient compte que des allitérations. Si les labiales *p, f, v* paraissent la marque du dédain, les assonances suggèrent parfaitement le contraste entre un lit 'rustique et clos' et un lit seigneurial: aux syllabes sourdes succèdent les mots clairs avec l'accumulation des *r* et des accents sonnant comme une fanfare (. . . *ment peint*/*d'or*, qui précèdent et suivent la césure).

> Hu*m*ble, ru*st*ique, et c*l*os, > ou *f*ier du pavill*o*n
> *Tr*iomphale*m*ent *p*eint d'*or* et de vermill*o*n. (p. 464)

La Mort de l'aigle

La Revue de Paris, 4 December 1864
The image of the eagle struck down by the storm, symbolizing the quick heroic death incurred by the ambitious idealist, has been well used in French poetry since at least the sixteenth century. Heredia's exploitation

of the theme's dramatic quality is very competent, even if we feel throughout the presence of Leconte de Lisle: the eagle leaves humanity and ordinary animals behind, rises higher and higher, meets the storm, is struck by a thunderbolt, spins and falls into the abyss, allowing the obvious reflective comparison to emerge in the climactic second tercet. The symbol had become commonplace even in Heredia's day and the poem now appears mechanically contrived for too obvious effect.

Plus ultra
Le Parnasse contemporain, 1876

The Latin phrase (meaning 'further' or 'beyond') which forms the title conveys the attraction entailed by the glorious conquest of the unknown. The symbol used here is a geographic one. Heredia's composition is again methodically dramatic. First, a preparation for the later climax by a kind of negative clearing away of what man has already conquered, the areas in the tropics, the Atlantic waters traversed by Western European galleons. In spirit and approach, 'Plus ultra' has much in common with the previous sonnet, 'La Mort de l'aigle'—*plus loin* here corresponding to *plus haut* in the previous poem. What draws him is a region well removed from all previous exploration, beyond the 'Ström' or maelstrom (whirl-pool near the Lofoten islands) and the barren 'Spitzbergs' (islands some 400 miles north of Lapland), and mention of such fearsome places is meant as proof enough of the forbidding isolation of his goal. The sestet introduces an obvious attempt to give vigour and immediacy by the hortative ('Partons!'). Lines 10–11 are very personal for Heredia. He is tired of the fame the *conquistadores* in the New World were able to gain, those men from whom he is descended. The abrupt future tense ('J'irai') stabs l. 12 more fiercely than 'Partons' did l. 9. He will climb the north-ernmost promontory in splendid loneliness. But the poem ends less fiercely than one might have expected. Again the sea is a friendly presence: its sound will give a comforting affirmation of his fame. The last line is the best in the sonnet. It is finely resonant by sound and mean-ing. 'Murmure de gloire' is original: 'gloire' would usually entail a much bolder, stronger, sound. The rhymes in ll. 9–10 are not good: a long, closed syllable with a short, open one.

La Vie des morts
Le Parnasse contemporain, 1876

The poem is dedicated to Armand Silvestre who, like Banville and other poets and artists of the time, favoured the pantheistic ideas present here. In Silvestre's book of poems *Les Renaissances* (1870), the first section was entitled 'La Vie des morts' and expressed the notions of the renewal of life through nature and of meeting and loving after death among the stars.

14. Poetry will bring together Heredia and Silvestre with many other fellow-spirits.

Au Tragédien E. Rossi

Unpublished before *Les Trophées*, 1893

Ernesto Rossi was famous for his acting in Shakespeare's plays, especially *Hamlet, Lear, Macbeth* and *Romeo and Juliet*. Heredia first saw him act in 1864, in Milan. An autograph copy (see Ibrovac, i, p. 236) makes it clear that the sonnet was composed in memory of the evenings in Venice in 1867 when Heredia, now with his wife, saw Rossi perform again and came to know him personally. 'Un des plus anciens [sonnets] et assurément le plus faible du recueil', says Ibrovac (ii, p. 482) and draws attention to the banality of the rhymes ('voir-soir', 'fer-enfer', 'flamme-âme'). The straining after dramatic effect is perhaps rendered more transparent and, seemingly, mechanical by the poem's anecdotic nature: first the intensive references to Rossi's acting in *Othello*, then in *Lear* and *Macbeth*, which, however impressively violent or moving, are there only to highlight the climax of his recitation of Dante. In the sestet, the alliterative consonants and resonant vowels undoubtedly impart vigour—'ta voix d'or', 'leur fanfare de fer', 'rouge du reflet de l'infernale flamme'—but the parenthetical clause in l. 13 seems mere padding.

10. *les trois rimes*: Dante's *terza rima*.

14. *Alighieri*: the name of Dante's family.

Michel-Ange

Revue des deux mondes, 1 February 1893

'Le Moyen Age et la Renaissance' would seem the appropriate section for this sonnet. Heredia admired the sculptor's work, though Michel-angelo is here mostly a symbol of the isolated artist who tries to defy death and time by rejecting vague yearning (l. 8) in favour of stubborn work—a Parnassian theme if ever there was one. Michelangelo's 'tragique tourment' (l. 1) is the anguish caused by the artist's longing to achieve perfect expression. In ll. 5–8, Heredia may be depicting Michel-angelo's destiny, which was to live through the disintegration of his country and the decadence of the arts in the later part of a career which had begun in the middle of the most brilliant period of the Renaissance. The sonnet's structure and the relationship between the octet and sestet hinge on the struggle of Michelangelo's spirit to express itself—visible in his creations and finally defeated by the intractability of matter.

1. *Certe*: see commentary for l. 9 of 'Blason céleste'; 'la Sixtine': the Sistine Chapel in the Vatican in Rome, with its famous frescos painted by Michelangelo, among them the Sibyls, the Prophets and the Last Judgement (ll. 3–4).

6. *Titan*: see commentary for 'La Naissance d'Aphrodite'. The rest of

the line is true both metaphorically and literally, since Michelangelo had to use high scaffolding to which he was tied in order to paint on the ceiling of the Sistine Chapel.

12. A typical contrast here—cf. 'froids . . . bout'—and an arresting fusion of opposites, the burning soul of the artist and the cold stone in which it is expressed.

Sur un Marbre brisé

La Légende du 'Parnasse contemporain', by C. Mendès, Bruxelles, Brancart, 1884

See the Introduction, p. 5.

The god is perhaps Terminus, Roman god of boundaries who was given the shape of a boundary stone surmounted by a bust (cf. l. 4, 'marqua les bornes'). But since the action of time has reduced the god's statue to 'ce débris divin', it is difficult to be sure. The octet's contrast is between the distant past, the time when the god's statue was intact and honoured with libations (l. 3) and the present, when its ruins lie amid the vigorous growth of hops, ivy and viburnum (l. 5). But l. 1 anticipates the sense of the tercet: moss has overgrown the statue's eyes, and this is a blessing, since it prevents the god from realizing how times have changed; the action of shade, leaves, sun and wind brings a greater kindness when they serve to give it new life. The earlier antithesis is worked into the climax's sharper contrasts: 'l'ombre errante' with 'le soleil qui bouge' (l. 13), 'ce marbre en ruine' with 'un Dieu vivant' (l. 14).

7. *Pan*: see commentary for 'Pan'. 'Faune': Roman god of the country-side. 'Hermès': Greek name for the Roman Mercury, son of Jupiter, messenger of the gods, god of eloquence, commerce and robbers. 'Silvain': Roman god of fields and forests, more or less equatable with the Greek Pan.

NOTES

INTRODUCTION

1. Mallarmé, Correspondance (1890–1891), iv, Gallimard, 1973, p. 582. Heredia mentions 'ce vaillant titre: *Les Trophées*' in a letter to Claudius Popelin, undated but probably late 1868, but it is not clear whether the reference is to a book planned by Popelin or to a book with that title by Heredia which Popelin would illustrate. See Joanna Richardson, 'José-Maria de Heredia: An Unpublished Correspondence', *Modern Language Review*, 65 (January 1970), 41.

2. Triptychs: 'Artémis'—'La Chasse'—'Nymphée'; 'Andromède au monstre'—'Persée et Andromède—'Le Ravissement d'Andromède'; 'Le Cydnus'—'Soir de bataille'—'Antoine et Cléopâtre'; 'La Vision de Khèm I, II, III'; the three poems of 'Romancero'; 'La Trebbia'—'Après Cannes'—'A un Triomphateur'; 'Suivant Pétrarque'—'Sur le livre des Amours de Pierre de Ronsard'—'La Belle Viole' (involving Du Bellay).
Diptychs: 'Némée'—'Stymphale': 'Nessus'—'La Centauresse': 'Centaures et Lapithes'—'Fuite de Centaures': 'Pan'—'Le Bain des nymphes': 'Le Chevrier'—'Les Bergers': 'Epigramme votive'—'Epigramme funéraire': 'Le Naufragé'—'La Prière du mort': 'La Jeune Morte'—'Regilla': 'Le Coureur'—'Le Cocher': 'Epiphanie'—'Le Huchier de Nazareth': 'Email'—'Rêves d'émail': 'Le Samouraï'—'Le Daïmio': 'Fleurs de feu' —'Fleur séculaire'.

3. From Coppée's reply to Heredia's *discours de réception* in the Académie française on 30 May 1895, Lemerre, 1895, p. 38.

4. These debts have been a happy hunting-ground for source-seekers like Ibrovac, who most thoroughly devoted a whole volume to them (see Bibliography). It would be quite beyond this edition's scope and purpose to give them all. My commentaries take up some of the more significant instances.

5. John C. Bailey, *The Claims of French Poetry*, London, Constable, 1907, p. 293.

6. In the sale catalogue of Heredia's library we can note the following: *L'Histoire de la Grèce* by G. Grote in 19 illustrated volumes, the *Histoire de la littérature grecque* by Otfried Muller and E. Burnouf, the works on comparative mythology by Max Müller, *L'Archéologie grecque* by Max. Collignon and the illustrated dictionaries by Smith and Antony Rich. (See Ibrovac, i, p. 248, note 3.)

7. Fernand Brodel, 'L'Elégie chez Heredia', *Mercure de France*, No. 532, 31ème année, tome cxlii, 15 August 1920, p. 121.

8. Eugène Langevin, 'José-Maria de Heredia—son œuvre poétique', *Le Correspondant*, 69ème année, 10 January 1907, pp. 72–3.

9. Like Joseph Vianey, 'Les Sonnets grecs de Heredia', *Revue des cours et conférences*, 19ème année (2ème série), No. 33, 21 June 1911, pp. 721–35, or Ibrovac, i, p. 247.

10. In *L'Evolution de la poésie lyrique en France au XIXème siècle*, tome i, p. 198, quoted by Vianey, op. cit., p. 722.

11. See Vianey, op. cit.

12. Vianey, op. cit., p. 723.

13. *Anthologie grecque*, traduite sur le texte publié d'après le manuscrit palatin par Fr. Jacobs [trans. F. Dehèque], Hachette, 1863, 2 vols.

14. See the *Anthologie grecque*, Introduction, p. 11.

15. Emile Zilliacus, '*José-Maria de Heredia et l'Anthologie grecque*', *Revue d'histoire littéraire de la France*, April–June 1910, pp. 1–9.

16. René Pichon, 'L'Antiquité romaine et la poésie française à l'époque parnassienne', *Revue des deux mondes*, 1 September 1911, p. 145.

17. Cf. the epigraphs of these sonnets.

18. Cf. Raoul Thauziès, 'Etude sur les sources de J.-M. de Heredia dans les cinquante-sept premiers sonnets des *Trophées*', *Revue des langues romanes*, 1910, tome liii, pp. 461–512 and 1911, tome liv, pp. 37–66.

19. Pichon, op. cit., p. 146.

20. See Gaston Deschamps, *La Vie et les livres*, 3ème série, Colin, 1896, p. 32.

21. See the letters exchanged between Heredia and Leconte de Lisle in Ibrovac, i, pp. 299–300.

22. Thus his library contained fifteen volumes on Japan and China.

23. Cf. Silvestre's collection of poems *Les Renaissances* (1870), divided into three sections: 'La Nature': 'Le Doute': 'Le Rêve'.

24. See the sonnet dedicated to Heredia which appeared with Heredia's 'Arvor' (later, 'Bretagne') in *La Vie moderne*, 23 July 1887, pp. 475–6.

25. *Rimes riches* are words having in common the *consonne d'appui* and two other elements, voiced consonant or vowel. Two *consecutive* rhyming vowels also count as *rime riche*, doubtless because this is a rare occurrence. *Rimes suffisantes* have two elements in common, *rimes pauvres* one. Defective rhymes are in 'Brise marine', ll. 1 and 4 and 'Plus ultra', ll. 9 and 10, both in 'La Nature et le rêve'. In fact, what many Parnassians sought was richness of rhyme and avoidance of banal, too obvious, rhymes; in this respect, Heredia was quite successful much of the time.

26. P. Valéry, 'Sur la technique littéraire', *Dossiers*, No. 1 (July 1946), pp. 27–8. The article was sent by Valéry to *Le Courrier libre* in 1889 but not published by that periodical.

SELECT BIBLIOGRAPHY

Abbreviations of works to which frequent reference is made are given after the work. Paris can be assumed as the place of publication for mentions of writings in French that do not specify place.

EDITIONS

Poésies complètes de Heredia, Les Trophées, sonnets et poèmes divers, texte définitif avec notes et variantes, Lemerre, 1924.

Los Trofeos, edited by José Antonio Niño, Universidad Nacional Autónoma de Mexico, 1957.

Los Trofeos (Sonetos), edited by Max Henriquez Ureña, Biblioteca Contemporánea, Editorial Losada, Buenos Aires, 1954.

CRITICISM

Bailey, John C., *The Claims of French Poetry*, London, Constable, 1907.

Brodel, Fernand, 'L'Elégie chez Heredia', *Mercure de France*, 15 August 1920.

Chisholm, A. R., 'A Secret of Heredia's Art', *Modern Language Review*, xxvi (April 1931), 159–67.

—, 'Towards an Analytical Criticism of Poetry', *Australian Universities Modern Language Association*, 22 (November 1964), 164–77.

Grammont, Maurice, *Le Vers français: ses moyens d'expression, son harmonie*, troisième édition revue et augmentée, Champion, 1923 (Grammont).

Harms, Alvin, *José-Maria de Heredia*, Boston, U.S.A., Twayne Publishers, 1975.

Ibrovac, Miodrag, *José-Maria de Heredia: sa vie—son œuvre*, Les Presses françaises, 1923, vol. i (Ibrovac, i), vol. ii (Ibrovac, ii).

—, *Les Sources des 'Trophées'*, Les Presses françaises, 1923 (Ibrovac, Sources).

Ince, W. N., *Heredia*, 'Athlone French Poets', The Athlone Press, 1979.

Langevin, Eugène, 'José-Maria de Heredia—son œuvre poétique', *Le Correspondant*, 10 January 1907.

Pichon, René, 'L'Antiquité romaine et la poésie française à l'époque parnassienne', *Revue des deux mondes*, 1 September 1911.

Secombe, Thomas and Brandin, Louis, 'José-Maria de Heredia, 1842–1905. The Evolution of the Sonnet', *The Fortnightly Review*, lxxviii (December 1905), 1074–87.

Thauziès, Raoul, 'Etude sur les sources des sonnets antiques de J.-M. de

Heredia', *Revue des langues romanes*, 1910, tome liii, pp. 461–512 and 1911, tome liv, pp. 37–66.

Vianey, Joseph, 'Les Sonnets grecs de Heredia', *Revue des cours et conférences*, 29 June 1911.

Zilliacus, Emile, 'José-Maria de Heredia et l'Anthologie grecque', *Revue d'histoire littéraire de la France*, April–June 1910.

SUGGESTIONS FOR FURTHER READING
OR CONSULTATION

Broome, Peter and Chesters, Graham, *The Appreciation of Modern French Poetry 1850–1950*, C.U.P., 1976 (see the introduction pp. 1–59 and its useful list of suggestions for further reading, pp. 60–1).

Delbouille, Paul, *Poésie et sonorités. La critique contemporaine devant le pouvir suggestif des sons*, Les Belles Lettres, 1961.

Deloffre, Frédéric, *Le Vers francais*, Société d'édition d'enseignement supérieur, 1973.

Gilman, Margaret, *The idea of poetry in France: from Houdar de la Motte to Baudelaire*, O.U.P., 1958.

Spire, André, *Plaisir poétique et plaisir musculaire*, Corti, 1949.